HONEST GRAFT

The World of
George Washington Plunkitt

HONEST GRAFT

The World of
George Washington Plunkitt

Plunkitt of Tammany Hall

A Series of Very Plain Talks on Very Practical Politics,
Delivered by Ex-Senator George Washington Plunkitt,
the Tammany Philosopher, from His Rostrum—
The New York County Court House Bootblack Stand

Recorded by
WILLIAM L. RIORDON
(1905)

WITH TWO ORIGINAL CONFLICTING INTERPRETATIONS
James S. Olson, *The World of George Washington Plunkitt*
James W. Mooney, *The Problem of the Cities Revisited*

BRANDYWINE PRESS • St. James, New York

Library of Congress Cataloging-in-Publication Data
Riordon, William L.
Honest Graft: The World of George Washington Plunkitt

ISBN: 1-881089-58-4

Plunkitt of Tammany Hall first published 1905
by E. P. Dutton & Co., Inc.

Honest Graft published 1993 by Brandywine Press

Telephone Orders: 1-800-345-1776

Second Edition - *Revised*

Contents

Part I

HONEST GRAFT: TWO VIEWS

The World of
George Washington Plunkitt

by
James S. Olson

George Washington Plunkitt was usually perched on the high chair of Anthony Graziano's shoeshine-bootblack stand in the old New York County Court-house—Tweed Courthouse—off Foley Square in New York City. From there he ruled one of the most lucrative political fiefdoms in the country. On cere-monial occasions, Plunkitt dressed up in a long, for-mal coat and top hat, but far more often than that he was high on his throne at Graziano's, decked out in shirtsleeves and suspenders, smoking an expen-sive cigar, looking out on New York City from under the shadow of a flat-topped, circular straw hat. It was 1903 and even though Plunkitt was a multimillion-aire, he came to Graziano's every day and expected a free shoeshine. Graziano was happy to oblige. A deal was a deal. George Washington Plunkitt made sure that Graziano's permit to keep the bootblack stand in front of the courthouse was renewed each year. In return, Plunkitt wanted his boots touched up regularly. One journalist was later to write that Plunkitt, on the bootblack stand, "received reports from his henchmen, distributed patronage, and adjusted complaints from his district. His filing cabinet was the sweatband on his hat."

Plunkitt was a living symbol of the rags-to-riches Horatio Alger story so many poor people yearned to fulfill. He had been born in 1842 in Nanny Goat Hill, a poor Irish shantytown on the upper west side of Manhattan, at a time when New Yorkers still grew crops in small patches of their yards and kept chickens and goats and even cows in makeshift sheds. Plunkitt's immigrant parents were dirt poor but they were dreamers. And the name they picked for their son was no coincidence. With a name like George Washington, they knew their boy was going to succeed in America. He did not make his fortune in business like Andrew Carnegie or John D. Rockefeller. George Washington Plunkitt made his money in politics. He was a Sachem of Tammany Hall.

When he was a boy, Plunkitt tired of school after "three winters of it" and went to work in a butcher shop. Year after year he came home tired and frustrated, his clothes covered in blood and his fingers cut up from accidental knife wounds, but he also learned the business, and in 1866 Plunkitt went off on his own, opening a butcher shop in Washington Square that soon prospered. But it was a limited prosperity—the good life that often comes to small businessmen who slave away in their shops for fifteen hours a day, seven days a week. Plunkitt wanted more, and one way for the son of Irish immigrants to grab more in America was politics.

Arriving during the Jacksonian era, when property barriers to voting had collapsed, the Irish became a powerful voting bloc. Lacking industrial skills, they were equipped with centuries of experience in life-or-death political battles with the English. In Ireland mass and direct action politics had gone on for years; and slowly, between 1820 and 1880, the Irish constructed their famous American political machines. Working with ethnic and religious unity through local Roman Catholic parishes and saloons, Irish politicians first became street captains and later district and precinct leaders, aldermen, and state and national legislators. Using police, fire department, sanitation, and public works jobs as patronage, they attracted the loyalty of voters economically dependent upon the political success of the machine. And by championing the workingman and the poor, Irish Catholic politicians became very influential in the Democratic Party. In Boston, Cleveland, Chicago, Pittsburgh, Baltimore, St. Louis, and New Orleans, Irish political machines were powerful, and power eventually translated into a shaky respectability. The premier symbol of Irish-American political power in the United States was New York's Tammany Hall.

Tammany Hall was the most powerful urban political machine in American history. William Mooney, a soldier during the American Revolution and a prominent anti-Federalist in New York City, had founded Tammany in 1789. He named the organization the Society of Saint Tammany, after a legendary Delaware Indian chief who supposedly concluded with William Penn the treaty handing all of Pennsylvania over to the Quakers. Naively hoping to become a national political movement, Tammany leaders organized thirteen "tribes," one in each of the thirteen states, and designated their leaders by such Indian titles as "Sachem" and "Sagamore." They called their meeting places "Wigwams." During its early years, Tammany was more of a fraternal organization than a political party, complete with oaths, covenants, secret grips and handshakes, and elaborate symbols whose meaning could be divined only by members.

By the early 1800s, Tammany Hall had all but disappeared except in New York City, where it became the organizational engine—the "machine"—driving the Democratic Party. Tammany was a kind of shadow government. More often than not its own members ran for political office, but even when Democrats who were not members of Tammany sought political office, they needed the backing of "The Hall." Otherwise, they did not have a prayer of being elected. The decades of Jeffersonian and Jacksonian Democracy in the early 1800s allowed Tammany to cloak itself in the robes of reform—supporting the campaign for manhood suffrage without property qualifications, calling for the abolition of debtors' prisons, and backing President Andrew Jackson in his righteous crusade against the Second Bank of the United States in 1832. Tammany assumed national political stature in 1836 when Martin Van Buren, the vice-president of the United States and its own Grand Sachem, was elected president of the United States.

Tammany Hall's seventy-year reign of political

dominance in New York City began in 1855 when Fernando Wood, one of its own, was elected mayor. Political opponents—particularly middle- and upper-class Republicans along with corporations—accused Wood and his cronies of graft and corruption, and those complaints reached a crescendo in 1868 when William Marcy "Boss" Tweed was elected Grand Sachem of Tammany. The new mayor—A. Oakey Hall—was little more than a Tweed stooge, and the Tweed Ring was charged with looting city coffers of $45 million and costing the city another $200 million in lost tax revenues through shady bond deals and by granting tax exemptions to individuals and businesses in return for kickbacks and political favors to the machine. Thomas Nast, the political cartoonist for *Harpers' Weekly*, drew a series of devastating, satirical cartoons of Tweed and his stooges, portraying the bosses as sleazy, greedy opportunists growing rich and fat at public expense. Samuel Jones Tilden, chairman of the New York State Democratic Party, launched an investigation of the Tweed Ring, and the sensational exposé of Tammany graft drove the Hall from power in 1871. Boss Tweed died in prison a few years later.

Tammany remained a potent force in city politics, however, and its banishment from the seat of power was only temporary. In 1874 John Kelly was elected Grand Sachem and Tammany regained control of city government. Richard Croker succeeded Kelly as Grand Sachem in 1886. Republicans resurrected their charges of graft and corruption over the years, and in 1894 the state legislature appointed the Lexow Commission to investigate charges of Tammany corruption. The heat was on again and Croker had to resign his Tammany post. A reform administration governed city politics for three years, but by 1897 Croker was back in charge of Tammany and Tammany was in charge of New York City. Seth Low, a progressive reformer, once again accused Tammany of political corruption, and in 1901 New York City voters rejected Tammany candidates. The divorce, however, lasted only two years. Charles Francis Murphy became Grand Sachem in 1902 and in 1903 voters returned Tammany to power.

For the next thirty years, Tammany Hall ruled New York City with an iron hand. Charles Murphy remained Grand Sachem until his death in 1924, when Judge George W. Olvany succeeded him. Jimmy Walker, the Tammany candidate, was elected mayor in 1926, but charges of corruption soon surfaced against him. Samuel Seabury led a state investigation of Tammany Hall, and the evidence of corruption was so overwhelming, and the news stories so sensational, that in 1932 Walker was forced to resign as mayor. Fiorello La Guardia, an anti-Tammany candidate for the Fusion Party, was elected mayor in 1933, and he remained in power for the next twelve years, wreaking havoc with Tammany Hall. The machine never regained its power, at least not as the dominating political force it had been from the mid-1850s to the early 1930s.

But during its seven-decade reign of power in New York City, Tammany Hall seemed to have more lives than the proverbial cat. Middle- and upper-class Republicans continually accused Tammany of buying votes, always insisting that New York City deserved better, that the good old boys down at the Hall should be turned out, that power should reside in those destined by breeding and education to rule— middle- and upper-class Republicans. Now and then, their accusations hit a responsive chord and voters sent Tammany a message, but the Hall always rose out of its ashes, working its political magic through the hundreds of thousands of working-class New Yorkers who were part of the organization.

What was most frustrating—at least to the upper classes—about Tammany Hall's political power was its quasi-legal status. The Tammany organization was unique among the major urban machines in the late nineteenth and early twentieth centuries. The reformers could never charge Tammany Hall with stealing an election by stuffing the ballot boxes with illegal votes. The Hall did not make it a continuing practice to register dead people and mark ballots for them; the Hall did not rely on getting its minions to vote two or three or four times; the Hall did not cheat when the votes were tallied. The Hall rarely stooped to voter fraud, for it did not need to. Tammany Hall enjoyed the genuine support of the people of New York City.

In 1901 Seth Low ousted Tammany in a reform crusade. Low had inherited a fortune from the family tea and silk importing business, but his real interest was good government. Elected twice as mayor of Brooklyn (1882–1885), Low emphasized efficiency, honesty, and merit in his administration of the city. He became president of Columbia University in 1889 and continued to promote the interests of reform in city government. Low left Columbia in 1901 when he decided to take on Tammany Hall and run for mayor of New York City. The campaign was a sensational one. Low accused Tammany of robbing the city blind, and he managed to win the election.

The next year Lincoln Steffens, managing editor of *McClure's Magazine*, began writing a series of exposés of corruption in American city government. One of his targets was Tammany Hall. The articles brought Steffens national attention, making him the most prominent muckraker in the United States, and formed the basis of his bestselling *The Shame of the Cities* in 1904. Steffens wrote: "Tammany is bad government; not inefficient, but dishonest; not a party, not a delusion and a snare, hardly known by its party name—Democracy; having little standing in the national councils of the party and caring little for influence outside of the city. Tammany is Tammany, the embodiment of corruption. All the world knows and all the world may know what it is and what it is after."

When Steffens was writing his essay on New York City, Tammany Hall was reasserting itself after its 1901 defeat. As far as Lincoln Steffens was concerned, Low had been the best of mayors—"conscientious and experienced and personally efficient" and New York City had the opportunity to show whether it had "that sustained good citizenship which alone can make democracy a success." The people of New York were going to decide whether they wanted good government or Tammany Hall. Seth Low thought he was a sure bet for a second term. The Fusion Party renominated him. Lincoln Steffens' revelations had excited the nation, and

Low's first-term had been a model of efficiency and honesty. He epitomized the reform spirit of the progressive era. The mayor thought he had brought good government to the city and believed that the people of New York City appreciated it. Tammany Hall nominated George B. McClellan to oppose Seth Low's candidacy. The election was not even close. McClellan won a 56 percent plurality, defeating Low by 314,782 votes to 252,086 votes. The people of New York City did not want good government or reform or efficiency or honesty or merit. They wanted Tammany Hall. Seth Low's defeat came as no surprise to Lincoln Steffens. He understood the system. In *The Shame of the Cities*, he wrote,

> Foreigners marvel . . . at us, and . . . cannot understand why we New Yorkers regard Tammany as so formidable. I think I can explain it. Tammany is corruption with consent; it is bad government founded on the suffrages of the people. . . . Tammany used to stuff the ballot boxes and intimidate voters; today there is practically none of that. Tammany rules . . . by right of the votes of the people of New York. Tammany corruption is democratic corruption. . . . Tammany's power is positive. . . . Tammany's democratic corruption rests upon the corruption of the people, the plain people, and there lies its great significance; its grafting system is one in which more individuals share than any I have studied.

Tammany's power rested on its ability to deliver. In 1870, when the population of New York City just exceeded one million people, Tammany Hall controlled nearly 14,000 municipal jobs. Later in the nineteenth century, when the city expanded geographically to include the Bronx, Queens, and Brooklyn, the population needing Tammany's service multiplied, but so did the volume of available resources. Although it is impossible to make any exact estimates, simple arithmetic throws some light on why Tammany enjoyed such extensive popular support even though its penchant for graft and corruption was widely known. If there were six members in the family—husband, wife, and four children—of each Tammany employee, then 84,000 people in the 1870s benefited directly, every day of the week, from the machine's power. To that number must be added thousands, perhaps even tens of thousands, of small businessmen like Anthony Graziano—bootblacks, pushcart operators, barbers, grocers, restaurant and cafe owners, taxi drivers, newspaper and magazine sellers, pharmacists, peddlars, and building contractors—who received licenses and exclusive concessions from the city. Those small businessmen and their families, as well as their employees and their employees' families, often viewed Tammany as a lifeline, a benefactor that kept them alive financially in a capricious economic world.

Beyond those hundreds of thousands of lower and working-class New Yorkers who saw a direct connection between their own welfare and that of Tammany Hall, there were tens of thousands of other New Yorkers who had been on the receiving end, more than once, of Tammany largesse—a turkey at Thanksgiving when the dinner table would have been empty otherwise, bail money for a son or father incarcerated for public intoxication or brawling after a night on the town, a pair of boots for a man about to start a new job, a hotel room for a family burned out of its house, a bucket of coal when there was no fuel in the oven, several boxes of groceries for new immigrants just off the boat from Europe, a casket and funeral for a dead child, a few dollars to pay a doctor's bill, or a good word to a banker or a loan shark or a bill collector about to get even with a poor family. At almost any time in the late nineteenth century and the early twentieth, most of the poor and working-class people of the city received what they considered real, tangible benefits from Tammany Hall. All Tammany asked in return was their votes.

Lincoln Steffens, even while condemning the corruption and autocracy he found in Tammany Hall, had a detached respect for the success of its democratic corruption, for the efficiency in which its leaders dispensed benefits to the multitudes:

> [T]he leader and his captains have their hold because they take care of their own. They speak pleasant words, smile friendly smiles, notice the baby, give picnics up the River or Sound, or a slap on the back; find jobs, most of them at city expense, but they have also newstands, peddling privileges, railroad and other business places to dispense; they permit violations of the law, and, if a man has broken the law without permission, see him through the court. Though a blow in the face is as readily given as a shake of the hand, Tammany kindness is real kindness, and will go far, remember long, and take infinite trouble for a friend.

Steffens also knew how Tammany defined friendship. A real friend, a true friend, was anybody who voted for Tammany Hall, who actively participated in the work to perpetuate the machine.

George Washington Plunkitt had been the most active of participants. From his butcher shop on Washington Square in the 1860s, he formed the George Washington Plunkitt Association, a group of people who agreed to cast their votes at his bidding. In return, Plunkitt made sure that they got the best cuts of pork or beef when they made their purchases, credit when they were short of cash, and even some free pork fat and soup bones when they were down and out. Soon the word was out around Washington Square that Plunkitt could deliver sixty votes. That attracted the interest of Tammany Hall. The head of the local election district named Plunkitt a "block captain"—head of the Tammany organization for one city block. The appointment gave him access to Tammany resources—the turkeys, bail money, coal, hotel rooms, or whatever he needed to assist "his" sixty voters. It was the beginning of a long, successful career for Plunkitt.

The Tammany Hall machine was an extraordinarily well-developed political organization. Its smallest unit was the tenement-house captain, the Tammany man within each working-class apartment house in the city. Twelve to fifteen tenement-house captains made up the block committee, headed by a block captain, and dozens of blocks formed an election district led by an election district committee and an election district captain. An assembly district, headed by an assembly leader and district committee, was composed of any number of election districts. The assembly district leaders had to stand for election in the

Democratic Party primaries, and they had the power to select the election district leaders. The district leaders together formed the county executive committee, which was headed by a chairman. At the top of it all was the Grand Sachem of Tammany Hall. By the early 1900s, when New York City included Manhattan, Staten Island, Queens, Brooklyn, and the Bronx, more than 32,000 people enjoyed formal political appointments at the election district committee level and above. With the addition of tenement-house captains and block committees, the number probably approached 100,000 people. It was an extraordinary political organization.

The opportunity to construct such an elaborate political machine in the United States was comparatively recent in origin. Early in the nineteenth century, American cities had been run by the Anglo-Protestant elites who owned property and who maintained their political power because poor and working-class people living in cities were not allowed to vote. Elite political values, and their economic corollaries, found expression in the National Republican Party of the 1820s, the Whig Party of the 1830s and 1840s, and the Republican Party in the 1850s. City services—public schools, road and bridge construction, water and sewage systems, garbage pick-up, and police and fire protection—all catered to the middle- and upper-class Anglo-Protestants.

But Jacksonian democracy and mass immigration from Europe undermined the urban political status quo. During the Age of Jackson, property requirements for voting disappeared state-by-state, allowing all white men to vote, including the lower classes.

The number of people casting ballots in city elections increased geometrically, and most of the new voters found their way to the Democratic Party, which was more sympathetic to their status. The same was true of the millions of immigrants who poured into the United States from Germany and Ireland in the nineteenth century. The Whig and later the Republican parties were unable to attract the loyalties of the new immigrants, primarily because many upper-class Anglo-Protestants were anti-Catholic nativists. In New York City, the immigrants turned to the Democratic Party for support, and Tammany Hall was only too happy to provide it. Within a generation, from the 1830s to the 1850s, the elite that had traditionally controlled New York City government found itself vastly outnumbered and politically overwhelmed by Tammany's supporters.

The Hall's ability to maintain the loyalties of so many people was directly connected to the physical growth of the city. Every year, beginning in the 1830s, thousands and then tens of thousands of new residents settled in New York City. They came from upstate New York, southern New England, and New Jersey farms, as well as from Ireland, Germany, and later Poland, Italy, Austria-Hungary, and Russia. The demand to house, feed, transport, educate, and protect these millions created a construction boom and a boom in city services that lasted throughout the nineteenth and into the twentieth century. Because the city either issued construction permits or directly contracted new building projects, there was a strong political component to the economic boom. Tammany Hall controlled the issuance of those building permits and construction contracts, as well as the tens of thousands of jobs associated with them. As George Washington Plunkitt remarked to journalist William Riordon in 1904, "I seen my opportunities and I took 'em." Take them he did. By the mid-1870s Plunkitt was a well-known Tammany Hall operative in the Fifteenth Assembly District around Washington Square. He was captain of an election district and knew that the city was about to begin construction of huge dock and wharf facilities in lower Manhattan. Plunkitt sold his butcher shop and used the capital to become a building contractor. These were the days before the era of competitive bidding, and Tammany Hall made sure that Plunkitt got his share of the projects, something befitting the needs of a powerful man on the make. Plunkitt himself made sure, of course, that all of his friends and his friends' friends got subcontracts and jobs on the projects. In 1868 he was elected to the state legislature, and in 1870 he began several terms as a city alderman. Plunkitt later bragged that he was the only person in New York City history to hold four different political offices at the same time—assemblyman, supervisor, alderman, and police magistrate. In 1883 Plunkitt won a seat in the state senate. Within a few years, George Washington Plunkitt was a millionaire and chairman of the Fifteenth Assembly District. The other Tammany assembly district chairmen—the exalted sachems—also became rich men.

The wealth of Tammany's leaders seemed illgotten gain to the Anglo-Protestant elites who had made their money on land in the early days of the republic or corporate profits in the industrial era. For them, the sleaziest form of scandal was exploiting political power and public office for personal gain. Self-righteous criticism of Tammany Hall corruption became the conventional wisdom of upper-class patricians and their voices in the intellectual community. In 1888 the British observer James Bryce, in his book *The American Commonwealth*, argued that "there is no denying that the government of cities is the one conspicuous failure of the United States." Andrew White, president of Cornell University, wrote in 1890 that "the city governments of the United States are the worst in Christendom—the most expensive, the most inefficient, and the most corrupt." In 1894 Edwin Godkin, editor of *The Nation*, declared that "the present condition of city governments in the United States is bringing democratic institutions into contempt the world over, and imperiling some of the best things in our civilization."

Since the times of the Founding Fathers in the late 1700s, Americans had been suspicious of political organizations. Classical democratic theory rejected the need for political parties of any kind, let alone organizational machines rich in resources. Citizens were expected to vote their consciences and to exercise the franchise directly, without the need for intermediaries between them and those they elected to serve. Tammany Hall seemed to contradict such high-minded values at every turn, and throughout its years of dominance in New York City, the Anglo-Protestant elites who had been driven from the seats of power raged against the Hall in self-righteous indignation, condemning machine politics as a "cancer of corruption" or a "moral depravity." Good government was detached and disinterested, efficient and fair, loyal to established procedures and regulations, with an educated electorate making rational choices about those who should govern them.

But what is rational to one person may not seem rational to another. Tammany Hall maintained its political control because it was eminently rational to most New York City voters. In the late nineteenth and early twentieth centuries, Tammany Hall was far more than a disinterested, detached city government for several million poor, working-class New Yorkers. It was also a successful city government delivering municipal services, a social welfare agency assisting the immigrant poor and their children in adjusting to the new country, a political interest group giving working-class people at least a modest voice in an economic world increasingly dominated by rich corporations, and a business with tens of thousands of employees.

In spite of the reform rhetoric, Tammany Hall was remarkably successful in managing the city's enormous growth. The New York City population increased from approximately 515,000 people in 1850 to more than seven million people in 1935. The city also expanded spatially, and its new residents demanded all the city services enjoyed by the people of central Manhattan—paved roads, street lights, electricity, water and sewage systems, fire and police protection, bridges, parks, libraries, schools, and public transportation. Tammany managed to supply those services. Historian Jon Teaford has argued that American cities in general—New York City included—enjoyed "as high a standard of public services as any urban residents in the world." In 1883 Tammany officials authorized a new Croton aqueduct system, and in 1905 they began developing the Catskill aqueduct, both of which gave New York City the finest water supply of any city on earth. Tammany built the bridges and tunnels—Brooklyn Bridge (1883), Williamsburg Bridge (1903), Manhattan Bridge (1909), Queensborough Bridge (1909), and Holland Tunnel (1927)—that linked Manhattan with New Jersey and Long Island. The organization completed Penn Station in 1910 and Grand Central Station in 1913. Tammany officials brought the elevated railroad and then the subway system to New York City.

By the 1920s, after more than a half-century of Tammany rule, New York City's system of public transportation, public education, and higher education was the envy of the world. And in spite of all the charges of mismanagement and corruption, Tammany managed to govern the city without ever declaring bankruptcy or defaulting on its obligations, even during the panics and depressions of 1873, 1893, and 1907. During Tammany's reign, New York City bonds enjoyed AAA ratings. The financial community considered them to be one of the best, safest, and most liquid investments in the world.

But Tammany was more than a political organization and a government to New York City residents, especially to the immigrant poor. During the years of Tammany power, millions arrived in New York City, Irish, Germans, Italians, Jews, Greeks, and African-Americans. By 1900, three out of four people in the city were either immigrants or the children of immigrants. For most of them, politics did not revolve around larger-than-life, complex issues like slavery or imperialism or free silver or civil service. Politics was tangible and personal, just as it had been in the Old World villages, where politicians were local people who could help you or hurt you. It was the same in New York City. When you had a problem, you took it to your block leader or election district chairman; all he wanted in return was your vote. Most Tammany leaders were second-generation Americans who understood the streets and the challenges of immigrant life. And poor people understood them. In an era when there were no formal government safety-net programs, Tammany acted as a social welfare agency to new immigrants. It was the purest form of representative government—local, responsive, and personal.

Tammany Hall was much more than a social welfare agency. It also served as an interest group—the only interest group—for a working class constituency. Between 1870 and 1920, virtually every section of American society, in attempts to cope with the industrial revolution, began to look outward and to form communities of interest. Businessmen established corporations to protect their capital, engaged in vertical and horizontal integration to increase profit margins, and established trade associations and groups like the Chamber of Commerce or the National Association of Manufacturers to promote their interests. Middle-class professionals formed organizations like the American Medical Association, the American Bar Association, or the American Dental Association. Eventually labor unions would emerge to perform the same services for workers, but unions—especially unions for mass production workers—were in their infancy in the late 1800s and early 1900s. Working class people confronted an increasingly organized economy without interest groups of their own. They were at the mercy of organized upper- and middle-class power brokers. What working-class people in New York City realized, however, was that those power brokers, if they were going to be successful economically, had to deal with Tammany Hall, and the sachems of the Hall would see to it that those benefits were widely distributed to the faithful.

Finally, Tammany Hall was a business, a big business, a way for talented, enterprising poor people to fulfill the American dream. Later generations would use sports and entertainment to get out of the ghetto; in the late 1800s and early 1900s, Tammany Hall was a way out. The city had an income of more than $100 million in 1904, and it spent that money providing services to its constituents. The sachems of Tammany Hall were its executives, the people who managed the business. They signed the contracts, controlled the cash flow, and watched the margins. They worked eighteen hour days, seven days a week, just like upper management businessmen today. And like the CEOs of the major corporations, they also took care of themselves, making the kind of money consistent with the huge operation they were running. Nobody expected them to live their city salaries. Over and over again, at every opportunity, Plunkitt used the inside information about impending city construction projects to make prudent investments or to demand kickbacks. He said disarmingly about the

system: "I don't think you can easily find a better example than I am of success in politics. After forty
years' experience at the game I am—well, I'm George
Washington Plunkitt. Everybody knows what figure I
cut in the greatest organization on earth, and if you
hear people say that I've laid away a million or so
since I was a butcher's boy in Washington Market,
don't come to me for an indignant denial. I'm pretty
comfortable, thank you."

Tammany Hall did not need to rig elections or steal
from the public treasury. Even Lincoln Steffens, one
of Tammany's most hostile critics, said that "hypocrisy is not a Tammany vice. Tammany is for Tammany, and the Tammany men say so. Other rings
proclaim lies and make pretensions; other rogues talk
about the tariff and imperialism. Tammany is honestly dishonest. Time and again, in private and in
public, the leaders, big and little, have said they are
out for themselves and their own. . . . Tammany
rules, when it rules, by right of the votes of the people of New York." This was honest graft. In the Declaration of Independence, Thomas Jefferson wrote
the noble words that government "derived its just
powers from the consent of the governed," but
George Washington Plunkitt said it even better:
"Tammany . . . looked after their friends, within the
law, and gave them what opportunities they could to
make honest graft. Now, let me tell you that's never
goin' to hurt Tammany with the people. Every good
man looks after his friends, and any man who
doesn't isn't likely to be popular. If I have a good
thing to hand out in private life, I give it to a friend.
Why shouldn't I do the same in public life?"

The Problem of the Cities Revisited

by
James W. Mooney

The modern American city is the creation of the country's technological and economic development. The cities that existed before the industrial revolution, although they might service important markets, were larger versions of the small, homogeneous communities in which the bulk of the nation's citizens lived. Industrialization and corporate growth brought staggering increases in urban population. Native workers, who were losing their farm jobs to the speedier efficiency of McCormick's mechanical reaper and other farm technology, rushed to the cities to fill the ranks of the new, largely unskilled urban proletariat in factories and shops. Along with the native-born workers were, of course, the immigrants. The relation between native workers and immigrant industrial laborers was uneasy: competition for jobs guaranteed that. And it was not long before the immigrant populations—first the Irish, then later in the nineteenth century Italians, Greeks, Russians, Jews, and others from lands mysterious to Americans— grew larger in number than the English, Scots, and Scots-Irish who had come to be considered of native stock. As early as 1880 immigrants made up as much as four-fifths of the population in some of the nation's largest cities. The hours they and natives worked were long, the conditions of work grinding and in many cases dangerous. Wages often no more than kept pace with the cost of living.

No one had planned the country's industrial revolution and no one had a plan for the development of the cities. The average city at the turn of the century was thick with problems, some of them familiar today.

Homelessness was common. Many lived in alleys, basements, or abandoned buildings, beside or beneath any structure that might afford some protection from the elements. Children without parents— "street arabs"—wandered at night in search of some sleeping place. Those among the working poor who could afford something better crowded into the filthy, disease-ridden tenements that Jacob Riis describes in *How the Other Half Lives* (1890). The middle classes, taking advantage of urban streetcars and, later, a rapid transit system, had begun to flee the deterioration of the central city for the peace and clean air of the suburbs. Suburban flight, then, was a phenomenon before it became identified with the mid-twentieth century.

One reason suburbanites gave for leaving was to escape the odors of the city. Baltimore smelled "like a billion polecats," complained or boasted that city's fond son H. L. Mencken. Pollution in industrial cities menaced health. Industrial and human waste was dumped carelessly by agencies and people with an uncertain understanding of proper sewage disposal. The engines of technology, the source of the nation's wealth and pride, could also cover a city with gas and smoke. The smoke from the oil, steel, and glass factories that operated around the clock in Pittsburgh was said to be so thick that people never saw the sun.

Crime haunted the nation's cities. And the complaints about it at the turn of the century have a remarkably present-day sound to them. Slums, then as now, were incubators of crime. "Incubators" is the right metaphor. Youth gangs roamed the streets of the country's major cities, usually at night, engaging in every form of criminal activity from petty theft to extortion and murder. New York's gangs were among those that took their names from the neighborhoods they "protected": Hell's Kitchen Boys, Poverty Gap, the Whyo Gang. In San Francisco the press used a new word, "hoodlums," to refer to the members of street gangs. Urban politicians were apparently not opposed to employing the gangs when it suited their purposes, especially during elections. The gangs rarely ventured beyond their own neighborhoods into the well-to-do sections of the city or beyond. A large portion of their victims were the immigrants, workers, and small shopkeepers with whom they shared the slums. Poverty in the late nineteenth century, as in the late twentieth, bred an underclass that preyed upon itself.

Prostitution flourished in the cities and there were always more than enough impoverished women, desperate to survive, to fill the brothels or opium dens. The number of homicides in the United States tripled in the 1880s; this was largely a measure of urban increase. Alcoholism was apparently on the rise during the same period and the number of saloons in Chicago, for example, began to rival that of food and clothing stores.

Crime, disease, pollution, squalid living conditions, addiction, hopelessness, all of which it is common to associate with cities today were part of the condition of the industrial city of the late nineteenth century. In the absence of any plan for urban development, dealing with the sordid conditions of urban growth was left to the city politicians and the organizations they constructed. Urban politics was the first response to the newly created problems of urban growth. And urban politics in the later nineteenth century meant boss politics and the political machine.

The modern American city was the product of the forces of industrialism and big business. So too was the city boss. Though its first appearance had been earlier, the big city machine took its more familiar form in the 1870s or eighties, mimicking the large businesses that had helped to create it. Like business, the machine existed to make a profit. Businesses made their profits by exchanging goods for money, and investing it; machines did so by exchanging jobs and services for power, and investing it. The bosses who ran the machines were remarkably similar to the buccaneering entrepreneurs of the early years of venture capitalism. Each in his own way was trying to make sense of powerful economic forces, each meant to replace with some system of order the chaos he found around him, and each aimed to make a profit for the effort.

The chaos of urban development in the late nineteenth century awakened a demand for a variety of urban services: housing, paved streets, sanitation, public utilities. In this situation, with its pressures for some sort of urban organization, the powerful city machine had an important place. The disorder of urban growth also increased the opportunities for corruption and greed.

The political techniques of the machines were essentially simple: in exchange for services the machine expected votes. A typical nineteenth-century American city was divided into wards or precincts. Each ward elected its own captain and each captain was responsible for his own constituency. The party machine connected these local officials under the leadership of the boss, who coordinated the activities of these officials through a system of patronage. In New York in the 1880s and nineties, Richard Croker, Honest John Kelly, and Charles F. Murphy led Tammany Hall, the Democratic party machine that controlled New York City politics until the 1930s and lingered in a weakened form for decades after. Christopher "Blind Boss" Buckley, who made up for failing eyesight with a keen ear for voices, ran San Francisco until reformers ousted him in 1891. In Cincinnati, George B. Cox ruled, in one critic's opinion, "as a medieval baron did his serfs." But perhaps the most notorious of the city bosses, not necessarily the strongest or the most corrupt but the recipient of the most publicity in his time, slightly preceded the great age of the machines: William Marcy Tweed, who headed the Tweed Ring in Tammany Hall from 1868 until his conviction for graft in 1873.

A great barrel of a man, Tweed had a reputation for being at home among the cultured elite and at ease in New York City's worst neighborhoods. He and his associates plundered the city treasury of almost $200 million. His behavior was conducted with the orderliness that a reformer craving efficiency might have admired. The Tweed Ring went about the business of graft with an accountant's energy. Bills were fattened by a fixed sum and kickbacks and payoffs were divided according to a plan in which Tweed's portion was always twenty percent.

Tweed's crowning piece of chicanery was the New York County Courthouse, The House that Tweed Built. Originally budgeted at a quarter of a million dollars, in the end the building cost the taxpayers over $13 million. Contractors had orders to pad their bills two or three times over a reasonable profit and return the difference to Tammany. The plasterer billed the city almost $3 million. Brooms cost over $40,000. When Tweed went to jail, the Courthouse was still unfinished.

The political machines devised a variety of services for drawing off the city's wealth and for keeping themselves in power. Control of the police allowed the more unscrupulous of the chieftains to preside over a network of profitable activities, including gambling, prostitution, and opium dens, that they afforded immunity in return for payoffs. Under the protection of Boss Boies Penrose, some of Philadelphia's most respected leaders collected rents on properties used as whorehouses. But the more common source of revenue came in the form of graft from contracts and franchises. And the tremendous growth of the cities in the last three decades of the century made for splendid opportunities for profit.

Tweed's Courthouse was the best known case of fraud. In Pittsburgh, which had a competitive bidding system for awarding contracts, almost all contracts went to one bidder, William Finn, one of the city's two bosses. Other politicians grew rich by receiving advance information on proposed municipal real estate purchases. George W. Plunkitt declared this "honest graft," for it was not a matter of actually "robbin' the city treasury."

The granting of franchises for public utilities— streetcars, gas works, electricity—were lucrative and often long-term sources of profits for those who contracted the allocation of city services. At the turn of the century utility corporations could be fiercely competitive and willing to pay out large sums in bribes or campaign contributions to officeholders. The Broadway Surface Railway dispersed almost a half a million dollars in bribes to city aldermen to win its contract. New York politicos were expert in the art of "sandbagging," a form of extortion that involved threatening city franchise holders by offering charters to competing firms.

So businessmen seeking stable profits in the highly combative world of late nineteenth-century capitalism poured money into city machines, which were as quick to sell influence to corporations as to provide jobs to voters. As New York's Richard Croker said, "Politics is business," a statement that might as easily have come from some business tycoon whose trade happened to be streetcars rather than votes.

The political equivalent of staying in business was staying in power and preserving the party machinery. Boss politics made use of patronage and the careful manipulation of elections. Party loyalists were given jobs, all at taxpayer expense, that required little or no actual work. One New York City ward captain was appointed to six municipal posts, none of which required much attention: together they fetched an annual $25,000. Keeping the party faithful employed also provided additional revenue for the party treasury. Employees on salary were expected to kick back to the party a share of their income; receivers of fees in their appointments might return to the machine a percentage of the charges. In one year in the 1870s Philadelphia tax collectors returned nearly a quarter of a million dollars to the gas-house ring that ran the city. Not all appointments, of course, were merely revenue producers for the holders and the machines. Perhaps most of the jobs that bosses controlled were in themselves honest and productive tasks, jobs that the poor were grateful to have and eager to repay in political loyalty. The repayment might not be at all in kickbacks: votes were a perfectly legal and, to a point, legitimate alternative. Tammany's 20,000 jobs, at any rate, were doubtless close to 20,000 cynical or genuinely grateful votes.

Votes, of course, were at the hub of the machinery. The patronage the party dispensed, the services it performed, and the jobs it arranged for the unemployed and needy were for the purpose of votes. Many of these votes were illegal or at least corrupt.

Politicians in virtually every major American city during the Gilded Age were guilty of ballot box stuffing, bribing voters, misplacing opposition votes, or some other form of manipulation. Tammany's Big Jim Sullivan used repeaters, unemployed men whom he would march, in various disguises, from one precinct to the next on election day to perform their repetitive duty for some extra cash or the price of a drink. Ballot fraud there was. But it was not what kept the machines in power. Just as barons in other lines of business sold real oil or real steel for real money, bosses sold real benefits—some of them in jobs, others in useful public services—for real votes. Bosses won elections because people voted for them. And people voted for them because in their way the bosses had been good for the voters.

Bosses were popular. They were popular at least among the large working-class and immigrant populations of the city, certainly more so than the genteel good-government reformers—the Goo-Goos, as the bosses called them—who periodically tried to cleanse government of the machines. Even urban reformers who managed to win office might put off the voters by their elitist demeanor and the coldly efficient governments they set up. It was not long before the bosses returned to power. "What tells in holdin' your grip on your district," said Plunkitt in one of his philosophical discourses on urban government, "is to go right down among the poor families and help them in the different ways they need help. . . . It's philanthropy, but it's politics, too—mighty good politics. . . . The poor are the most grateful people in the world." Bosses and their lieutenants passed out

Christmas turkeys, and they provided coal on especially harsh winter days. It was a good precinct captain who treated constituents to a holiday picnic with
some kegs of beer or helped when a family needed
some extra groceries or sent a gift to welcome a birth
or a spray of flowers to mourn a death. In the immigrant wards some Yiddish, a few words in Italian,
and a little of the Gaelic went a long way. Boss politics at its most attractive, and it was often at its most
attractive, combined services with friendliness and
suggested, not falsely, that the bosses and captains
themselves were of the urban culture to which they
ministered.

Americans love an outlaw. Feeling compressed
within networks of restraints, rules written and un-
written, they take some vicarious pleasure in the
exploits and the freedom of the rebel. Nothing else
will account for the icons of our popular culture who
never seem so heroic or attractive as when they press
the limits of conventional behavior. They voyage like
our primal national hero Huck Finn at the fringes of
civilization, or invent themselves like the grainy private investigators of the movies and television. Practical sense too suggests that layering regulation upon
regulation makes for gridlock. The bosses had neither
the innocence of Huck nor the shabby nobility of a
Bogart character. But they had their own easy way
with respectability. And at a time when the city was
expanding uncontrollably and there were no guide-
lines to follow, no clear channels of authority and responsibility, those flamboyant chieftains were able to
get things done. A city job lowered the unemploy-
ment numbers by one, and a bucket of coal warmed

one more room, at a time when WPA projects and rent subsidies were not available to do more and a scrupulous politics would have done less. That the bosses often took something in return, even looted, or engaged in honest graft was only to be expected from people who made no secret of their appetites and took a certain pride in scandalous behavior. Wage workers, immigrants, and urban bosses shared a perspective of themselves as outsiders in a largely middle-class Protestant world.

That machine politics expressed a rough democracy was in effect the finding of the most famous enemy of bossism, Lincoln Steffens, in muckraking articles collected in *The Shame of the Cities*. Steffens was no starchy defender of privileged respectability: he became an authentic social radical. But his indictment of the cities was neo-republican. The evil, he believed, had to do less with the sins of the bosses than with the degradation of the mass of people who lacked the courage and will to govern themselves. Urban decay went not from the top down but from the bottom up. It was a matter of original sin. For the bold rapacity of the city politician, a figure of a muscularity the populace lacked, Steffens expressed some admiration. The boss was a crook but "a great crook" and "a character . . . to know intimately and be proud of."

What, then, was so very wrong with boss politics? City bossism was corrupt. Other forms of politics are clean? And are governments set up for the purpose of being clean: institutions expressly committed, as some reformers appear to have thought, to the project of cultivating their own purity? Bossism brought tangible benefits to people afflicted with a poverty, distant from the society of Goo-Goos and progressives, that some bosses and their lieutenants certainly had undergone or at least seen in the constituents among whom they moved. What, under the circumstances, would day laborers and tenement dwellers have gained from the replacement of machine politics with a politics of reform, efficiency, and rigorous administration?

A brief answer is that bossism did nearly nothing to address the fundamental ills that plagued American cities. Machine politicos, of course, were capable of better things. Alfred E. Smith, cultivated as a servant of Tammany, became a major progressive reformer; and doubtless his own brushes with youthful deprivation, in an upbringing on the streets that nurtured countless machine loyalists, contributed to his angry espousal of social legislation. But it was common for bosses and captains to share in the predatory hunger of the business leaders who were their twin products of the age's economics, and often enough their partners in plunder. That is no argument for reform, unless the reformers offered something more than efficiency and chilly rectitude. Did they?

The first of the reformers did not do so, or more precisely were unable to articulate whatever projects beyond efficiency and honesty may have moved them. One group of Gilded Age reformers known as mugwumps, taken from a northeastern Indian term for a great man, aimed to end urban corruption through civil service reform. Located mostly in the cities of the Northeast and especially in New England, representing the conservative and educated upper classes, the mugwumps had a concept of political leadership that suggests the old Puritan patriarchy: solid, wise, prosperous beyond temptation. The effect of the patronage system, the mugwumps argued, was to put into office a class suited neither by learning nor by social standing to the demands of office, beholden to the party machine and to the business interests that fed the machine, incapable of statesmanlike independence. The mugwump program intended to take officeholding outside the control of the electorate, the urban voters who were manipulated by politicians, consigning it instead to a system of civil-service examinations that would select the ablest people. Honesty and efficiency would flourish under the guidance of an aristocracy civic minded and knowledgeable of the real needs of the city.

Although the mugwumps enjoyed some small successes in reorganizing the structures of municipal government, most city offices remained appointive and therefore political. The stiff patrician morality of the good-government reformers offended the public. In condemning the ethnic politics of city bosses and the seduction of the city's immigrant populations, reformers sounded like denouncing the habits and customs of the ethnic groups the machines claimed to champion. Chilled by the icy virtue of the reformers, immigrants preferred the warm-blooded politics of the bosses. Good-government administrations rarely lasted more than one term. They were like "mornin' glories," said Plunkitt. Bright early in the day, they dried up by night. The machines went "flourishin' forever, like fine old oaks." The reason reformers fared so poorly, Plunkitt offered, was that they did not understand politics as a profession, did not know how to work the wards and precincts. If anything was going either successfully or usefully to replace bossism, it would have to have more to say to city folk than the good-government advocates.

Then, around and before the turn of the twentieth century, just such a challenge appeared in the person of a new kind of political boss, the reform mayor. The social justice mayors, as they have been called, included Detroit's Hazen Pingree, Cleveland's Tom L. Johnson, and from Toledo Sam "Golden Rule" Jones, so named for his dedication to that command. Most had made fortunes operating city businesses before they turned to politics. They aimed at creating more stable and rational municipal management, but in the interest of energetic programs of social democracy.

Reform mayors worked at regularizing city services, imposing tighter controls on urban corporations, modernizing tax systems, or some combination. Almost all embarked on public works projects, which might include schools, hospitals, and sanitation programs, along with parks, public baths, and recreational facilities. In the rough and tumble of the nation's cities they conducted a practical politics, often using the tactics of the bosses they were trying to replace, compounding personal philanthropy with party machinery. It was reform, but reform bossism.

Another serious competitor to the machines, also offering the public something real, was the reform spirit of the early twentieth century known then and now as progressivism. Among the many impulses, some of them conflicting, within progressivism, that most relevant to the cities was the faith in scientific and scholarly expertise and in government by continuing administration. Like bossism, which had its likeness in big business, progressive urban reform reflected major economic and productive forces of its time. The increasingly compelling scientific and technological triumphs of industrialism inspired among city reformers a conviction that expert knowledge could address itself to urban problems and advanced administration could solve them. The scientific reformers shared with the mugwumps an elitist notion of government. But while the good-government people had looked to the traditional patrician class or at any rate to the institutions that defined it, progressives wanted an elite of specialized professional training. The social-justice mayors, coming just before or at the beginning of the progressive era, had done little to disrupt the brawling energy of urban democratic politics. They simply adopted it to their own reform purposes. They often employed experts in urban management—engineers, statisticians, public-health specialists, and economists among others; but these, instead of taking the place of elective processes, were supposed to effect the will of the voters. Scientific progressives shifted the balance. They spoke to urban problems in a way that mugwumps had not effectively done. But in their vision of expert administration, they advocated government not by continual popular will but by city managers or city commissions, government by urban specialists and trained administrators either appointed or chosen in at-large elections. Scientific management would thicken the distance between government and the electorate.

Some progressive reformers wanted a democracy limited to the solid citizenry, the reflective voter. The unreflective and ill-informed electorate they worked to exclude through literacy tests and strict voter registration laws. Some, moreover, favored trimming services for the sake of efficiency and economy. Yet the motive was not parsimony but a quest of lean effectiveness. Government by scientific management was capable of allying itself with major projects of social and economic justice. Al Smith, for many years a fighter for social democratic reforms in New York state, drew heavily on the advice of experts; and as governor he worked to limit the number of state elective offices, believing that an administration appointed by an executive responsible to the electorate would make for the best kind of democratic governance.

Such, in short, are the contrasts in aim and method between the bosses and the reformers of various kinds. Underlying them is at least an implicit difference between the bosses and the reformers, more particularly those who came after the mugwumps, in the understanding of human nature as it expresses itself in social and political life. In essence: the machine politicos, for all their genuine resonance with their constituencies, saw the average voter as a creature of appetite (the bosses, after all, knew appetite at first hand); the scientific progressives, for all their hauteur, expected something better of the public and were prepared to work for it.

The posture on the part of the bosses toward their clients is reflected in their attitude toward poverty. Even Plunkitt's self-advertising could not hide the cynicism and condescension of his reference to the poor as "the most grateful people in the world." As long as the grateful poor were poor, the bosses were empowered. Poverty contributed to a perverted patriarchy in which "the poor look up to George W. Plunkitt as a father," explained that political metaphysician, "come to him in trouble—and don't forget him on election day." It would be unfair to accuse the bosses and captains of consciously feeding on poverty or its attendant attitudes. But they refused to give the least consideration to origins.

Progressives treated the city as a social force that could negate the will of its inhabitants. In the statistics and urban surveys compiled by scientific social workers and city planners, reformers had developed an environmentalism that challenged their own inherited notions of human agency and responsibility. They became aware of how the forces of the city converged on its inhabitants and shaped their lives, aware of the power and impersonality of the organic city in creating poverty. As Edward Devine, head of the New York Charity Organization Society, expressed it in 1909: "personal depravity is as foreign to any theory of the hardships of our modern poor as witchcraft or demonical possession. . . . These hardships are economic, social, transitional, measurable, manageable." Reformers meant, then, to build up countervailing powers in the form of administrative institutions to oppose the enormous force of the organic city and urban poverty.

Proceeding on either the city or the state level according to the issue at hand, progressives committed themselves to providing for schools, parks, and hospitals, for child labor laws, factory safety regulation, and workers' compensation, and for what may seem a quixotic humanization of the city through such activities as the "City Beautiful" movement. The urban beautifiers laid out plans that incorporated magnificently landscaped boulevards with easy means of transportation, a careful balance of working and living spaces, and a dense packing of parks and museums and other forms of aesthetic activity. Architect and pioneering urban planner Daniel Hudson Burnham, chief designer of Chicago's world fair of 1893 that served as the inspiration for the City-Beautiful vision, laid out a plan for that city that included slum clearance, a transportation and sanitation system, and the construction of a park, museum, and recreational facilities along the lakefront. His design moved residents to centers of government and employment along arteries of broad streets graced with cultural and recreational facilities. Large pieces of the Burnham plan were adopted and helped to earn for Chicago the reputation, for a time, of "The City That Works."

There was nothing intentionally demeaning in the progressive definition of poverty as a force that shapes the will of the poor. The progressives did not have in mind a simple behaviorism. They did not reduce human beings to mere bundles of behavioral responses to external stimuli: that way of perceiving human nature was more typical of the bosses with their systems of massive bribery. But they understood the intricate connections between self-mastery and mastery of society. The problem is to bring about the circumstances in which self-mastery and a virtuous citizenry can thrive. That means releasing people from the deadening constrictions of poverty. It also means constructing a forum for intelligent popular political discourse. This the reformers set about to do by establishing civic associations and municipal leagues, public spaces for the discussion of issues. Bosses exchanged benevolence for votes and left the habits of their constituents undisturbed; reformers fashioned cities at once more compassionate and more demanding of private virtue and civic responsibility.

Reformers took seriously the problem of political morality that will not go away. The political machines actually anticipated a more recent politics that severs moral from political life and assumes that the flashy, self-aggrandizing politician expresess both the character and the desires of the people. Progressives rejected the conviction that private appetites should define the public interest. By any reasonable standard of political virtue, a George Washington Plunkitt was a greater threat to the health of the community than a William Tweed. Tweed can at least be credited with recognizing corruption for what it is: he used graft as a means to illicit wealth and he engaged in public works to hide his crimes. Plunkitt believed that he was committing no sin, that what he did by means foul or fair was consonant with the morality, if that is the word, of the rest of the people. The modern parallel to Plunkitt's defense of "honest graft" is Nixon's plaintive cry, in the midst of the Watergate revelations, that he was not a crook.

In describing American urban development, the historian Richard Hofstadter has observed that somewhere around the turn of the century a nation born in the country moved to the city. It might be said of the United States in these past couple of decades that a nation reared in the cities has moved back to the country, or to the country manqué, the suburbs. For the moment the epicenter of political concern has shifted away from the cities and away from massive government support for urban projects. As inner-city tax bases erode and urban superstructures decay, the temptation is to give the city over to the local demagogue who promises hugely and delivers nothing. In the meaner times of a troubled economy shadowed by a gigantic national debt, cities will need to rely more than ever on the skills and talents of their leaders not simply for urban management but for instilling in city populations, including their more prosperous sections, a sense of a need for sharing and common sacrifice. What the reformers believed is applicable today: that in the life of a city, or a republic, moral economy is as essential as political economy. Enthroned in his seat at Graziano's shoeshine stand in the New York County Courthouse counting out the benefits of "honest graft," Plunkitt of Tammany Hall would have found no more substance to that claim than to the gray twists of smoke curling up from the tip of his cigar. George Plunkitt may have known his constituents intimately, as he so often said. He just didn't have very much respect for them.

Part II

PLUNKITT OF TAMMANY HALL

Preface

THIS volume discloses the mental operations of perhaps the most thoroughly practical politician of the day—George Washington Plunkitt, Tammany leader of the Fifteenth Assembly District, Sachem of the Tammany Society and Chairman of the Elections Committee of Tammany Hall, who has held the offices of State Senator, Assemblyman, Police Magistrate, County Supervisor and Alderman, and who boasts of his record in filling four public offices in one year and drawing salaries from three of them at the same time.

The discourses that follow were delivered by him from his rostrum, the bootblack stand in the County Courthouse, at various times in the last half-dozen years. Their absolute frankness and vigorous unconventionality of thought and expression charmed me. Plunkitt said right out what all practical politicians think but are afraid to say. Some of the discourses I published as interviews in the *New York Evening Post*, the *New York Sun*, the *New York World*, and the *Boston Transcript*. They were reproduced in newspapers throughout the country and several of them, notably the talks on "The Curse of Civil Service Reform" and "Honest Graft and Dishonest Graft," became subjects of discussion in the United States Senate and in college lectures. There seemed to be a general recognition of Plunkitt as a striking type of the practical politician, a politician, moveover, who dared to say publicly what others in his class whisper among themselves in the City Hall corridors and the hotel lobbies.

I thought it a pity to let Plunkitt's revelations of himself—as frank in their way as Rousseau's *Confessions*—perish in the files of the newspapers; so I collected the talks I had published, added several new ones, and now give to the world in this volume a system of political philosophy which is as unique as it is refreshing.

No New Yorker needs to be informed who George Washington Plunkitt is. For the information of others, the following sketch of his career is given. He was born, as he proudly tells, in Central Park—that is, in the territory now included in the park. He began life as a driver of a cart, then became a butcher's boy, and later went into the butcher business for himself. How he entered politics he explains in one of his discourses. His advancement was rapid. He was in the Assembly soon after he cast his first vote and has held office most of the time for forty years.

In 1870, through a strange combination of circumstances, he held the places of Assemblyman, Alderman, Police Magistrate and County Supervisor and drew three salaries at once—a record unexampled in New York politics.

Plunkitt is now a millionaire. He owes his fortune mainly to his political pull, as he confesses in "Honest Graft and Dishonest Graft." He is in the contracting, transportation, real estate, and every other business out of which he can make money. He has no office. His headquarters is the County Courthouse bootblack stand. There he receives his constituents, transacts his general business and pours forth his philosophy.

Plunkitt has been one of the great powers in Tammany Hall for a quarter of a century. While he was in the Assembly and the State Senate he was one of the most influential members and introduced the bills that provided for the outlying parks of New York City, the Harlem River Speedway, the Washington Bridge, the 155th Street Viaduct, the grading of Eighth Avenue north of Fifty-seventh Street, additions to the Museum of Natural History, the West Side Court, and many other important public improvements. He is one of the closest friends and most valued advisers of Charles F. Murphy, leader of Tammany Hall.

WILLIAM L. RIORDON

A Tribute to Plunkitt
by the Leader
of Tammany Hall

SENATOR PLUNKITT is a straight organization man. He believes in party government; he does not indulge in cant and hypocrisy and he is never afraid to say exactly what he thinks. He is a believer in thorough political organization and all-the-year-around work, and he holds to the doctrine that, in making appointments to office, party workers should be preferred if they are fitted to perform the duties of the office. Plunkitt is one of the veteran leaders of the organization; he has always been faithful and reliable, and he has performed valuable services for Tammany Hall.

CHARLES F. MURPHY

Honest Graft
and Dishonest Graft

EVERYBODY is talkin' these days about Tammany men growin' rich on graft, but nobody thinks of drawin' the distinction between honest graft and dishonest graft. There's all the difference in the world between the two. Yes, many of our men have grown rich in politics. I have myself. I've made a big fortune out of the game, and I'm gettin' richer every day, but I've not gone in for dishonest graft—blackmailin' gamblers, saloonkeepers, disorderly people, etc.—and neither has any of the men who have made big fortunes in politics.

There's an honest graft, and I'm an example of how it works. I might sum up the whole thing by sayin': "I seen my opportunities and I took 'em."

Just let me explain by examples. My party's in power in the city, and it's goin' to undertake a lot of public improvements. Well, I'm tipped off, say, that they're going to lay out a new park at a certain place.

I see my opportunity and I take it. I go to that place and I buy up all the land I can in the neighborhood. Then the board of this or that makes its plan public, and there is a rush to get my land, which nobody cared particular for before.

Ain't it perfectly honest to charge a good price and make a profit on my investment and foresight? Of course, it is. Well, that's honest graft.

Or supposin' it's a new bridge they're goin' to build. I get tipped off and I buy as much property as I can that has to be taken for approaches. I sell at my own price later on and drop some more money in the bank.

Wouldn't you? It's just like lookin' ahead in Wall Street or in the coffee or cotton market. It's honest graft, and I'm lookin' for it every day in the year. I will tell you frankly that I've got a good lot of it, too.

I'll tell you of one case. They were goin' to fix up a big park, no matter where. I got on to it, and went lookin' about for land in that neighborhood.

I could get nothin' at a bargain but a big piece of swamp, but I took it fast enough and held on to it. What turned out was just what I counted on. They couldn't make the park complete without Plunkitt's swamp, and they had to pay a good price for it. Anything dishonest in that?

Up in the watershed I made some money, too. I bought up several bits of land there some years ago and made a pretty good guess that they would be bought up for water purposes later by the city.

Somehow, I always guessed about right, and shouldn't I enjoy the profit of my foresight? It was rather amusin' when the condemnation commissioners came along and found piece after piece of the land in the name of George Plunkitt of the Fifteenth Assembly District, New York City. They wondered how I knew just what to buy. The answer is—I seen my opportunity and I took it. I haven't confined myself to land; anything that pays is in my line.

For instance, the city is repavin' a street and has several hundred thousand old granite blocks to sell. I am on hand to buy, and I know just what they are worth.

How? Never mind that. I had a sort of monopoly of this business for a while, but once a newspaper tried to do me. It got some outside men to come over from Brooklyn and New Jersey to bid against me.

Was I done? Not much. I went to each of the men and said: "How many of these 250,000 stones do you want?" One said 20,000, and another wanted 15,000, and another wanted 10,000. I said: "All right, let me bid for the lot, and I'll give each of you all you want for nothin'."

They agreed, of course. Then the auctioneer yelled: "How much am I bid for these 250,000 fine pavin' stones?"

"Two dollars and fifty cents," says I.

"Two dollars and fifty cents!" screamed the auctioneer. "Oh, that's a joke! Give me a real bid."

He found the bid was real enough. My rivals stood silent. I got the lot for $2.50 and gave them their share. That's how the attempt to do Plunkitt ended, and that's how all such attempts end.

I've told you how I got rich by honest graft. Now, let me tell you that most politicians who are accused of robbin' the city get rich the same way.

They didn't steal a dollar from the city treasury. They just seen their opportunities and took them. That is why, when a reform administration comes in and spends a half million dollars in tryin' to find the public robberies they talked about in the campaign, they don't find them.

The books are always all right. The money in the city treasury is all right. Everything is all right. All they can show is that the Tammany heads of departments looked after their friends, within the law, and gave them what opportunities they could to make honest graft. Now, let me tell you that's never goin' to hurt Tammany with the people. Every good man looks after his friends, and any man who doesn't isn't likely to be popular. If I have a good thing to hand out in private life, I give it to a friend. Why shouldn't I do the same in public life?

Another kind of honest graft. Tammany has raised a good many salaries. There was an awful howl by the reformers, but don't you know that Tammany gains ten votes for every one it lost by salary raisin'?

The Wall Street banker thinks it shameful to raise a department clerk's salary from $1500 to $1800 a year, but every man who draws a salary himself says: "That's all right. I wish it was me." And he feels very much like votin' the Tammany ticket on election day, just out of sympathy.

Tammany was beat in 1901 because the people were deceived into believin' that it worked dishonest graft. They didn't draw a distinction between dishonest and honest graft, but they saw that some Tammany men grew rich, and supposed they had been robbin' the city treasury or levyin' blackmail on disorderly houses, or workin' in with the gamblers and lawbreakers.

As a matter of policy, if nothing else, why should the Tammany leaders go into such dirty business, when there is so much honest graft lyin' around when they are in power? Did you ever consider that?

Now, in conclusion, I want to say that I don't own a dishonest dollar. If my worst enemy was given the job of writin' my epitaph when I'm gone, he couldn't do more than write:

"George W. Plunkitt. He Seen His Opportunities, and He Took 'Em."

How to Become
a Statesman

THERE's thousands of young men in this city who will
go to the polls for the first time next November.
Among them will be many who have watched the
careers of successful men in politics, and who are
longin' to make names and fortunes for themselves
at the same game. It is to these youths that I want to
give advice. First, let me say that I am in a position to
give what the courts call expert testimony on the subject. I don't think you can easily find a better example
than I am of success in politics. After forty years' experience at the game I am—well, I'm George Washington Plunkitt. Everybody knows what figure I cut
in the greatest organization on earth, and if you hear
people say that I've laid away a million or so since
I was a butcher's boy in Washington Market, don't
come to me for an indignant denial. I'm pretty comfortable, thank you.

Now, havin' qualified as an expert, as the lawyers

say, I am goin' to give advice free to the young men
who are goin' to cast their first votes, and who are
lookin' forward to political glory and lots of cash.
Some young men think they can learn how to be successful in politics from books, and they cram their
heads with all sorts of college rot. They couldn't
make a bigger mistake. Now, understand me, I ain't
sayin' nothin' against colleges. I guess they'll have to
exist as long as there's bookworms, and I suppose
they do some good in a certain way, but they don't
count in politics. In fact, a young man who has gone
through the college course is handicapped at the out-
set. He may succeed in politics, but the chances are
100 to 1 against him.

Another mistake: some young men think that the
best way to prepare for the political game is to practice speakin' and becomin' orators. That's all wrong.
We've got some orators in Tammany Hall, but they're
chiefly ornamental. You never heard of Charlie Murphy delivering a speech, did you? Or Richard Croker,
or John Kelly, or any other man who has been a real
power in the organization? Look at the thirty-six district leaders of Tammany Hall today. How many of
them travel on their tongues? Maybe one or two, and
they don't count when business is doin' at Tammany
Hall. The men who rule have practiced keepin' their
tongues still, not exercisin' them. So you want to
drop the orator idea unless you mean to go into politics just to perform the skyrocket act.

Now, I've told you what not to do; I guess I can explain best what to do to succeed in politics by tellin'
you what I did. After goin' through the apprentice-
ship of the business while I was a boy by workin'

around the district headquarters and hustlin' about the polls on election day, I set out when I cast my first vote to win fame and money in New York City politics. Did I offer my services to the district leader as a stump-speaker? Not much. The woods are always full of speakers. Did I get up a book on municipal government and show it to the leader? I wasn't such a fool. What I did was to get some marketable goods before goin' to the leaders. What do I mean by marketable goods? Let me tell you: I had a cousin, a young man who didn't take any particular interest in politics. I went to him and said: "Tommy, I'm goin' to be a politician, and I want to get a followin'; can I count on you?" He said, "Sure, George." That's how I started in business. I got a marketable commodity— one vote. Then I went to the district leader and told him I could command two votes on election day, Tommy's and my own. He smiled on me and told me to go ahead. If I had offered him a speech or a bookful of learnin', he would have said, "Oh, forget it!"

That was beginnin' business in a small way, wasn't it? But that is the only way to become a real lastin' statesman. I soon branched out. Two young men in the flat next to mine were school friends. I went to them, just as I went to Tommy, and they agreed to stand by me. Then I had a followin' of three voters and I began to get a bit chesty. Whenever I dropped into district headquarters, everybody shook hands with me, and the leader one day honored me by lightin' a match for my cigar. And so it went on like a snowball rollin' down a hill. I worked the flat-house that I lived in from the basement to the top floor, and I got about a dozen young men to follow me. Then I tackled the next house and so on down the block and around the corner. Before long I had sixty men back of me, and formed the George Washington Plunkitt Association.

What did the district leader say then when I called at headquarters? I didn't have to call at headquarters. He came after me and said: "George, what do you want? If you don't see what you want, ask for it. Wouldn't you like to have a job or two in the departments for your friends?" I said: "I'll think it over; I haven't yet decided what the George Washington Plunkitt Association will do in the next campaign." You ought to have seen how I was courted and petted then by the leaders of the rival organizations. I had marketable goods and there was bids for them from all sides, and I was a risin' man in politics. As time went on, and my association grew, I thought I would like to go to the Assembly. I just had to hint at what I wanted, and three different organizations offered me the nomination. Afterwards, I went to the Board of Aldermen, then to the State Senate, then became leader of the district, and so on up and up till I became a statesman.

That is the way and the only way to make a lastin' success in politics. If you are goin' to cast your first vote next November and want to go into politics, do as I did. Get a followin', if it's only one man, and then go to the district leader and say: "I want to join the organization. I've got one man who'll follow me through thick and thin." The leader won't laugh at your one-man followin'. He'll shake your hand warmly, offer to propose you for membership in his club, take you down to the corner for a drink and ask you to call again. But go to him and say: "I took first prize at college in Aristotle; I can recite all Shakespeare forwards and backwards; there ain't nothin' in science that ain't as familiar to me as blockades on the elevated roads and I'm the real thing in the way of silver-tongued orators." What will he answer? He'll probably say: "I guess you are not to blame for your misfortunes, but we have no use for you here."

The Curse of
Civil Service Reform

THIS civil service law is the biggest fraud of the age. It
is the curse of the nation. There can't be no real patriotism while it lasts. How are you goin' to interest our
young men in their country if you have no offices to
give them when they work for their party? Just look
at things in this city today. There are ten thousand
good offices, but we can't get at more than a few hundred of them. How are we goin' to provide for the
thousands of men who worked for the Tammany
ticket? It can't be done. These men were full of patriotism a short time ago. They expected to be servin'
their city, but when we tell them that we can't place
them, do you think their patriotism is goin' to last?
Not much. They say: "What's the use of workin' for
your country anyhow? There's nothin' in the game."
And what can they do? I don't know, but I'll tell
you what I do know. I know more than one young
man in past years who worked for the ticket and was

just overflowin' with patriotism, but when he was knocked out by the civil service humbug he got to hate his country and became an Anarchist. This ain't no exaggeration. I have good reason for sayin' that most of the Anarchists in this city today are men who ran up against civil service examinations. Isn't it enough to make a man sour on his country when he wants to serve it and won't be allowed unless he answers a lot of fool questions about the number of cubic inches of water in the Atlantic and the quality of sand in the Sahara desert? There was once a bright young man in my district who tackled one of these examinations. The next I heard of him he had settled down in Herr Most's saloon smokin' and drinkin' beer and talkin' socialism all day. Before that time he had never drank anything but whisky. I knew what was comin' when a young Irishman drops whisky and takes to beer and long pipes in a German saloon. That young man is today one of the wildest Anarchists in town. And just to think! He might be a patriot but for that cussed civil service.

Say, did you hear about that Civil Service Reform Association kickin' because the tax commissioners want to put their fifty-five deputies on the exempt list, and fire the outfit left to them by Low? That's civil service for you. Just think! Fifty-five Republicans and mug-wumps holdin' $3000 and $4000 and $5000 jobs in the tax department when 1555 good Tammany men are ready and willin' to take their places! It's an outrage! What did the people mean when they voted for Tammany? What is representative government, anyhow? Is it all a fake that this is a government of the people, by the people and for the people? If it isn't a fake, then why isn't the people's voice obeyed and Tammany men put in all the offices?

When the people elected Tammany, they knew just what they were doin'. We didn't put up any false pretenses. We didn't go in for humbug civil service and all that rot. We stood as we have always stood, for rewardin' the men that won the victory. They call that the spoils system. All right; Tammany is for the spoils system, and when we go in we fire every anti-Tammany man from office that can be fired under the law. It's an elastic sort of law and you can bet it will be stretched to the limit. Of course the Republican State Civil Service Board will stand in the way of our local Civil Service Commission all it can; but say!— suppose we carry the State sometime, won't we fire the upstate Board all right? Or we'll make it work in harmony with the local board, and that means that Tammany will get everything in sight. I know that the civil service humbug is stuck into the constitution, too, but, as Tim Campbell said: "What's the constitution among friends?"

Say, the people's voice is smothered by the cursed civil service law; it is the root of all evil in our government. You hear of this thing or that thing goin' wrong in the nation, the State or the city. Look down beneath the surface and you can trace everything wrong to civil service. I have studied the subject and I know. The civil service humbug is underminin' our institutions and if a halt ain't called soon this great republic will tumble down like a Park Avenue house when they were buildin' the subway, and on its ruins will rise another Russian government.

This is an awful serious proposition. Free silver

and the tariff and imperialism and the Panama Canal are triflin' issues when compared to it. We could worry along without any of these things, but civil service is sappin' the foundation of the whole shootin' match. Let me argue it out for you. I ain't up on sillygisms, but I can give you some arguments that nobody can answer.

First, this great and glorious country was built up by political parties; second, parties can't hold together if their workers don't get the offices when they win; third, if the parties go to pieces, the government they built up must go to pieces, too; fourth, then there'll be h——— to pay.

Could anything be clearer than that? Say, honest now; can you answer that argument? Of course you won't deny that the government was built up by the great parties. That's history, and you can't go back of the returns. As to my second proposition, you can't deny that either. When parties can't get offices, they'll bust. They ain't far from the bustin' point now, with all this civil service business keepin' most of the good things from them. How are you goin' to keep up patriotism if this thing goes on? You can't do it. Let me tell you that patriotism has been dying out fast for the last twenty years. Before then when a party won, its workers got everything in sight. That was somethin' to make a man patriotic. Now, when a party wins and its men come forward and ask for their rewards, the reply is, "Nothin' doin', unless you can answer a list of questions about Egyptian mummies and how many years it will take for a bird to wear out a mass of iron as big as the earth by steppin' on it once in a century!"

I have studied politics and men for forty-five years, and I see how things are driftin'. Sad indeed is the change that has come over the young men, even in my district, where I try to keep up the fire of patriotism by gettin' a lot of jobs for my constituents, whether Tammany is in or out. The boys and men don't get excited any more when they see a United States flag or hear "The Star-Spangled Banner." They don't care no more for firecrackers on the Fourth of July. And why should they? What is there in it for them? They know that no matter how hard they work for their country in a campaign, the jobs will go to fellows who can tell about the mummies and the bird steppin' on the iron. Are you surprised then that the young men of the country are beginnin' to look coldly on the flag and don't care to put up a nickel for firecrackers?

Say, let me tell of one case. After the battle of San Juan Hill, the Americans found a dead man with a light complexion, red hair and blue eyes. They could see he wasn't a Spaniard, although he had on a Spanish uniform. Several officers looked him over, and then a private of the Seventy-first Regiment saw him and yelled, "Good Lord, that's Flaherty." That man grew up in my district, and he was once the most patriotic American boy on the West Side. He couldn't see a flag without yellin' himself hoarse.

Now, how did he come to be lying dead with a Spanish uniform on? I found out all about it, and I'll vouch for the story. Well, in the municipal campaign of 1897, that young man, chockful of patriotism, worked day and night for the Tammany ticket. Tammany won, and the young man determined to devote his life to the service of the city. He picked out a place that would suit him, and sent in his application to the head of department. He got a reply that he must take a civil service examination to get the place. He didn't know what these examinations were, so he went, all lighthearted, to the Civil Service Board. He read the questions about the mummies, the bird on the iron, and all the other fool questions—and he left that office an enemy of the country that he had loved so well. The mummies and the bird blasted his patriotism. He went to Cuba, enlisted in the Spanish army at the breakin' out of the war, and died fightin' his country.

That is but one victim of the infamous civil service. If that young man had not run up against the civil examination, but had been allowed to serve his country as he wished, he would be in a good office today, drawin' a good salary. Ah, how many young men have had their patriotism blasted in the same way!

Now, what is goin' to happen when civil service crushes out patriotism? Only one thing can happen: the republic will go to pieces. Then a czar or a sultan will turn up, which brings me to the fourthly of my argument—that is, there will be h——— to pay. And that ain't no lie.

Reformers
Only Mornin' Glories

COLLEGE professors and philosophers who go up in a balloon to think are always discussin' the question: "Why Reform Administrations Never Succeed Themselves!" The reason is plain to anybody who has learned the a, b, c of politics.

I can't tell just how many of these movements I've seen started in New York during my forty years in politics, but I can tell you how many have lasted more than a few years—none. There have been reform committees of fifty, of sixty, of seventy, of one hundred and all sorts of numbers that started out to do up the regular political organizations. They were mornin' glories—looked lovely in the mornin' and withered up in a short time, while the regular machines went on flourishin' forever, like fine old oaks. Say, that's the first poetry I ever worked off. Ain't it great?

Just look back a few years. You remember the People's Municipal League that nominated Frank Scott for mayor in 1890? Do you remember the reformers that got up that league? Have you ever heard of them since? I haven't. Scott himself survived because he had always been a first-rate politician, but you'd have to look in the newspaper almanacs of 1891 to find out who made up the People's Municipal League. Oh, yes! I remember one name: Ollie Teall; dear, pretty Ollie and his big dog. They're about all that's left of the League.

Now take the reform movement of 1894. A lot of good politicians joined in that—the Republicans, the State Democrats, the Stecklerites and the O'Brienites, and they gave us a lickin', but the real reform part of the affair, the Committee of Seventy that started the thing goin', what's become of those reformers? What's become of Charles Stewart Smith? Where's Bangs? Do you ever hear of Cornell, the iron man, in politics now? Could a search party find R. W. G. Welling? Have you seen the name of Fulton McMahon or McMahon Fulton—I ain't sure which—in the papers lately? Or Preble Tucker? Or—but it's no use to go through the list of the reformers who said they sounded in the death knell of Tammany in 1894. They're gone for good, and Tammany's pretty well, thank you. They did the talkin' and posin', and the politicians in the movement got all the plums. It's always the case.

The Citizens' Union has lasted a little bit longer than the reform crowd that went before them, but that's because they learned a thing or two from us. They learned how to put up a pretty good bluff—and bluff counts a lot in politics. With only a few thousand members, they had the nerve to run the whole Fusion movement, make the Republicans and other organizations come to their headquarters to select a ticket and dictate what every candidate must do or not do. I love nerve, and I've had a sort of respect for the Citizens' Union lately, but the Union can't last. Its people haven't been trained to politics, and whenever Tammany calls their bluff they lay right down. You'll never hear of the Union again after a year or two.

And, by the way, what's become of the good government clubs, the political nurseries of a few years ago? Do you ever hear of Good Government Club D and P and Q and Z any more? What's become of the infants who were to grow up and show us how to govern the city? I know what's become of the nursery that was started in my district. You can find pretty much the whole outfit over in my headquarters, Washington Hall.

The fact is that a reformer can't last in politics. He can make a show for a while, but he always comes down like a rocket. Politics is as much a regular business as the grocery or the dry-goods or the drug business. You've got to be trained up to it or you're sure to fail. Suppose a man who knew nothing about the grocery trade suddenly went into the business and tried to conduct it according to his own ideas. Wouldn't he make a mess of it? He might make a splurge for a while, as long as his money lasted, but his store would soon be empty. It's just the same with a reformer. He hasn't been brought up in the difficult business of politics and he makes a mess of it every time.

I've been studyin' the political game for forty-
five years, and I don't know it all yet. I'm learnin'
somethin' all the time. How, then, can you expect
what they call "business men" to turn into politics
all at once and make a success of it? It is just as if I
went up to Columbia University and started to teach
Greek. They usually last about as long in politics as I
would last at Columbia.

You can't begin too early in politics if you want to
succeed at the game. I began several years before I
could vote, and so did every successful leader in
Tammany Hall. When I was twelve years old I made
myself useful around the district headquarters and
did work at all the polls on election day. Later on, I
hustled about gettin' out voters who had jags on or
who were too lazy to come to the polls. There's a
hundred ways that boys can help, and they get an experience that's the first real step in statesmanship.
Show me a boy that hustles for the organization on
election day, and I'll show you a comin' statesman.

That's the a, b, c of politics. It ain't easy work to get
up to y and z. You have to give nearly all your time
and attention to it. Of course, you may have some
business or occupation on the side, but the great
business of your life must be politics if you want to
succeed in it. A few years ago Tammany tried to mix
politics and business in equal quantities, by havin'
two leaders for each district, a politician and a business man. They wouldn't mix. They were like oil and
water. The politician looked after the politics of his
district; the business man looked after his grocery
store or his milk route, and whenever he appeared
at an executive meeting, it was only to make trouble.

The whole scheme turned out to be a farce and was abandoned mighty quick.

Do you understand now, why it is that a reformer goes down and out in the first or second round, while a politician answers to the gong every time? It is because the one has gone into the fight without trainin', while the other trains all the time and knows every fine point of the game.

New York City Is Pie for the Hayseeds

THIS city is ruled entirely by the hayseed legislators at Albany. I've never known an upstate Republican who didn't want to run things here, and I've met many thousands of them in my long service in the Legislature. The hayseeds think we are like the Indians to the National Government—that is, sort of wards of the State, who don't know how to look after ourselves and have to be taken care of by the Republicans of St. Lawrence, Ontario, and other backwoods counties. Why should anybody be surprised because ex-Governor Odell comes down here to direct the Republican machine? Newburg ain't big enough for him. He, like all the other upstate Republicans, wants to get hold of New York City. New York is their pie.

Say, you hear a lot about the downtrodden people of Ireland and the Russian peasants and the sufferin' Boers. Now, let me tell you that they have more real freedom and home rule than the people of this grand

and imperial city. In England, for example, they make a pretense of givin' the Irish some self-government. In this State the Republican government makes no pretense at all. It says right out in the open: "New York City is a nice big fat Goose. Come along with your carvin' knives and have a slice." They don't pretend to ask the Goose's consent.

We don't own our streets or our docks or our waterfront or anything else. The Republican Legislature and Governor run the whole shootin' match. We've got to eat and drink what they tell us to eat and drink, and have got to choose our time for eatin' and drinkin' to suit them. If they don't feel like takin' a glass of beer on Sunday, we must abstain. If they have not got any amusements up in their backwoods, we mustn't have none. We've got to regulate our whole lives to suit them. And then we have to pay their taxes to boot.

Did you ever go up to Albany from this city with a delegation that wanted anything from the Legislature? No? Well, don't. The hayseeds who run all the committees will look at you as if you were a child that didn't know what it wanted, and will tell you in so many words to go home and be good and the Legislature will give you whatever it thinks is good for you. They put on a sort of patronizing air, as much as to say, "These children are an awful lot of trouble. They're wantin' candy all the time, and they know that it will make them sick. They ought to thank goodness that they have us to take care of them." And if you try to argue with them, they'll smile in a pityin' sort of way as if they were humorin' a spoiled child.

But just let a Republican farmer from Chemung or Wayne or Tioga turn up at the Capital. The Republican Legislature will make a rush for him and ask him what he wants and tell him if he doesn't see what he wants to ask for it. If he says his taxes are too high, they reply to him: "All right, old man, don't let that worry you. How much do you want us to take off?"

"I guess about fifty per cent will about do for the present," says the man. "Can you fix me up?"

"Sure," the Legislature agrees. "Give us somethin' harder, don't be bashful. We'll take off sixty per cent if you wish. That's what we're here for."

Then the Legislature goes and passes a law increasin' the liquor tax or some other tax in New York City, takes a half of the proceeds for the State Treasury and cuts down the farmers' taxes to suit. It's as easy as rollin' off a log—when you've got a good workin' majority and no conscience to speak of.

Let me give you another example. It makes me hot under the collar to tell about this. Last year some hayseeds along the Hudson River, mostly in Odell's neighborhood, got dissatisfied with the docks where they landed their vegetables, brickbats, and other things they produce in the river counties. They got together and said: "Let's take a trip down to New York and pick out the finest dock we can find. Odell and the Legislature will do the rest." They did come down here, and what do you think they hit on? The finest dock in my district. Invaded George W. Plunkitt's district without sayin' as much as "by your leave." Then they called on Odell to put through a bill givin' them this dock, and he did.

When the bill came before Mayor Low I made the greatest speech of my life. I pointed out how the Legislature could give the whole waterfront to the hayseeds over the head of the Dock Commissioner in the same way, and warned the Mayor that nations had rebelled against their governments for less. But it was no go. Odell and Low were pards and—well, my dock was stolen.

You heard a lot in the State campaign about Odell's great work in reducin' the State tax to almost nothin', and you'll hear a lot more about it in the campaign next year. How did he do it? By cuttin' down the expenses of the State Government? Oh, no! The expenses went up. He simply performed the old Republican act of milkin' New York City. The only difference was that he nearly milked the city dry. He not only ran up the liquor tax, but put all sorts of taxes on corporations, banks, insurance companies, and everything in sight that could be made to give up. Of course, nearly the whole tax fell on the city. Then Odell went through the country districts and said: "See what I have done for you. You ain't got any more taxes to pay the State. Ain't I a fine feller?"

Once a farmer in Orange County asked him: "How did you do it, Ben?"

"Dead easy," he answered. "Whenever I want any money for the State Treasury, I know where to get it," and he pointed toward New York City.

And then all the Republican tinkerin' with New York City's charter. Nobody can keep up with it. When a Republican mayor is in, they give him all sorts of power. If a Tammany mayor is elected next fall I wouldn't be surprised if they changed the whole business and arranged it so that every city department should have four heads, two of them Republicans. If we make a kick, they would say: "You don't know what's good for you. Leave it to us. It's our business."

To Hold Your District: Study Human Nature and Act Accordin'

THERE's only one way to hold a district: you must study human nature and act accordin'. You can't study human nature in books. Books is a hindrance more than anything else. If you have been to college, so much the worse for you. You'll have to unlearn all you learned before you can get right down to human nature, and unlearnin' takes a lot of time. Some men can never forget what they learned at college. Such men may get to be district leaders by a fluke, but they never last.

To learn real human nature you have to go among the people, see them and be seen. I know every man, woman, and child in the Fifteenth District, except them that's been born this summer—and I know some of them, too. I know what they like and what they don't like, what they are strong at and what they are weak in, and I reach them by approachin' at the right side.

For instance, here's how I gather in the young men. I hear of a young feller that's proud of his voice, thinks that he can sing fine. I ask him to come around to Washington Hall and join our Glee Club. He comes and sings, and he's a follower of Plunkitt for life. Another young feller gains a reputation as a baseball player in a vacant lot. I bring him into our baseball club. That fixes him. You'll find him workin' for my ticket at the polls next election day. Then there's the feller that likes rowin' on the river, the young feller that makes a name as a waltzer on his block, the young feller that's handy with his dukes— I rope them all in by givin' them opportunities to show themselves off. I don't trouble them with political arguments. I just study human nature and act accordin'.

But you may say this game won't work with the high-toned fellers, the fellers that go through college and then join the Citizens' Union. Of course it wouldn't work. I have a special treatment for them. I ain't like the patent medicine man that gives the same medicine for all diseases. The Citizens' Union kind of a young man! I love him! He's the daintiest morsel of the lot, and he don't often escape me.

Before telling you how I catch him, let me mention that before the election last year, the Citizens' Union said they had four hundred or five hundred enrolled voters in my district. They had a lovely headquarters, too, beautiful roll-top desks and the cutest rugs in the world. If I was accused of havin' contributed to fix up the nest for them, I wouldn't deny it under oath. What do I mean by that? Never mind. You can guess from the sequel, if you're sharp.

Well, election day came. The Citizens' Union's candidate for Senator, who ran against me, just polled five votes in the district, while I polled something more than 14,000 votes. What became of the 400 or 500 Citizens' Union enrolled voters in my district? Some people guessed that many of them were good Plunkitt men all along and worked with the Cits just to bring them into the Plunkitt camp by election day. You can guess that way, too, if you want to. I never contradict stories about me, especially in hot weather. I just call your attention to the fact that on last election day 395 Citizens' Union enrolled voters in my district were missin' and unaccounted for.

I tell you frankly, though, how I have captured some of the Citizens' Union's young men. I have a plan that never fails. I watch the City Record to see when there's civil service examinations for good things. Then I take my young Cit in hand, tell him all about the good thing and get him worked up till he goes and takes an examination. I don't bother about him any more. It's a cinch that he comes back to me in a few days and asks to join Tammany Hall. Come over to Washington Hall some night and I'll show you a list of names on our rolls marked "C.S." which means, "bucked up against civil service."

As to the older voters, I reach them, too. No, I don't send them campaign literature. That's rot. People can get all the political stuff they want to read—and a good deal more, too—in the papers. Who reads speeches, nowadays, anyhow? It's bad enough to listen to them. You ain't goin' to gain any votes by stuffin' the letter boxes with campaign documents. Like as not you'll lose votes for there's nothin' a man hates more than to hear the letter carrier ring his bell and go to the letter box expectin' to find a letter he was lookin' for, and find only a lot of printed politics. I met a man this very mornin' who told me he voted the Democratic State ticket last year just because the Republicans kept crammin' his letter box with campaign documents.

What tells in holdin' your grip on your district is to go right down among the poor families and help them in the different ways they need help. I've got a regular system for this. If there's a fire in Ninth, Tenth, or Eleventh Avenue, for example, any hour of the day or night, I'm usually there with some of my election district captains as soon as the fire engines. If a family is burned out I don't ask whether they are Republicans or Democrats, and I don't refer them to the Charity Organization Society, which would investigate their case in a month or two and decide they were worthy of help about the time they are dead from starvation. I just get quarters for them, buy clothes for them if their clothes were burned up, and fix them up till they get things runnin' again. It's philanthropy, but it's politics, too—mighty good politics. Who can tell how many votes one of these fires bring me? The poor are the most grateful people in the world, and, let me tell you, they have more friends in their neighborhoods than the rich have in theirs.

If there's a family in my district in want I know it before the charitable societies do, and me and my men are first on the ground. I have a special corps to look up such cases. The consequence is that the poor look up to George W. Plunkitt as a father, come to him in trouble—and don't forget him on election day.

Another thing, I can always get a job for a deservin' man. I make it a point to keep on the track of jobs, and it seldom happens that I don't have a few up my sleeve ready for use. I know every big employer in the district and in the whole city, for that matter, and they ain't in the habit of sayin' no to me when I ask them for a job.

And the children—the little roses of the district! Do I forget them? Oh, no! They know me, every one of them, and they know that a sight of Uncle George and candy means the same thing. Some of them are the best kind of vote-getters. I'll tell you a case. Last year a little Eleventh Avenue rosebud, whose father is a Republican, caught hold of his whiskers on election day and said she wouldn't let go till he'd promise to vote for me. And she didn't.

On *The Shame*
of the Cities

I'VE been readin' a book by Lincoln Steffens on *The Shame of the Cities*. Steffens means well but, like all reformers, he don't know how to make distinctions. He can't see no difference between honest graft and dishonest graft and, consequent, he gets things all mixed up. There's the biggest kind of a difference between political looters and politicians who make a fortune out of politics by keepin' their eyes wide open. The looter goes in for himself alone without considerin' his organization or his city. The politician looks after his own interests, the organization's interests, and the city's interests all at the same time. See the distinction? For instance, I ain't no looter. The looter hogs it. I never hogged. I made my pile in politics, but, at the same time, I served the organization and got more big improvements for New York City than any other livin' man. And I never monkeyed with the penal code.

The difference between a looter and a practical politician is the difference between the Philadelphia Republican gang and Tammany Hall. Steffens seems to think they're both about the same; but he's all wrong. The Philadelphia crowd runs up against the penal code. Tammany don't. The Philadelphians ain't satisfied with robbin' the bank of all its gold and paper money. They stay to pick up the nickels and pennies and the cop comes and nabs them. Tammany ain't no such fool. Why, I remember, about fifteen or twenty years ago, a Republican superintendent of the Philadelphia almshouse stole the zinc roof off the buildin' and sold it for junk. That was carryin' things to excess. There's a limit to everything, and the Philadelphia Republicans go beyond the limit. It seems like they can't be cool and moderate like real politicians. It ain't fair, therefore, to class Tammany men with the Philadelphia gang. Any man who undertakes to write political books should never for a moment lose sight of the distinction between honest graft and dishonest graft, which I explained in full in another talk. If he puts all kinds of graft on the same level, he'll make the fatal mistake that Steffens made and spoil his book.

A big city like New York or Philadelphia or Chicago might be compared to a sort of Garden of Eden, from a political point of view. It's an orchard full of beautiful apple trees. One of them has got a big sign on it, marked: "Penal Code Tree—Poison." The other trees have lots of apples on them for all. Yet the fools go to the Penal Code Tree. Why? For the reason, I guess, that a cranky child refuses to eat good food and chews up a box of matches with relish. I never had any temptation to touch the Penal Code Tree.

The other apples are good enough for me, and O Lord! how many of them there are in a big city!

Steffens made one good point in his book. He said he found that Philadelphia, ruled almost entirely by Americans, was more corrupt than New York, where the Irish do almost all the governin'. I could have told him that before he did any investigatin' if he had come to me. The Irish was born to rule, and they're the honestest people in the world. Show me the Irishman who would steal a roof off an almhouse! He don't exist. Of course, if an Irishman had the political pull and the roof was much worn, he might get the city authorities to put on a new one and get the contract for it himself, and buy the old roof at a bargain—but that's honest graft. It's goin' about the thing like a gentleman, and there's more money in it than in tearin' down an old roof and cartin' it to the junkman's—more money and no penal code.

One reason why the Irishman is more honest in politics than many Sons of the Revolution is that he is grateful to the country and the city that gave him protection and prosperity when he was driven by oppression from the Emerald Isle. Say, that sentence is fine, ain't it? I'm goin' to get some literary feller to work it over into poetry for next St. Patrick's Day dinner.

Yes, the Irishman is grateful. His one thought is to serve the city which gave him a home. He has this thought even before he lands in New York, for his friends here often have a good place in one of the city departments picked out for him while he is still in the old country. Is it any wonder that he has a tender spot in his heart for old New York when he is on its salary list the mornin' after he lands?

Now, a few words on the general subject of the so-called shame of cities. I don't believe that the government of our cities is any worse, in proportion to opportunities, than it was fifty years ago. I'll explain what I mean by "in proportion to opportunities." A half a century ago, our cities were small and poor. There wasn't many temptations lyin' around for politicians. There was hardly anything to steal, and hardly any opportunities for even honest graft. A city could count its money every night before goin' to bed, and if three cents was missin', all the fire bells would be rung. What credit was there in bein' honest under them circumstances? It makes me tired to hear of old codgers back in the thirties or forties boastin' that they retired from politics without a dollar except what they earned in their profession or business. If they lived today, with all the existin' opportunities, they would be just the same as twentieth-century politicians. There ain't any more honest people in the world just now than the convicts in Sing Sing. Not one of them steals anything. Why? Because they can't. See the application?

Understand, I ain't defendin' politicians of today who steal. The politician who steals is worse than a thief. He is a fool. With the grand opportunities all around for the man with a political pull, there's no excuse for stealin' a cent. The point I want to make is that if there is some stealin' in politics, it don't mean that the politicians of 1905 are, as a class, worse than them of 1835. It just means that the old-timers had nothin' to steal, while the politicians now are surrounded by all kinds of temptations and some of them naturally—the fool ones—buck up against the penal code.

Ingratitude in Politics

THERE'S no crime so mean as ingratitude in politics, but every great statesman from the beginnin' of the world has been up against it. Caesar had his Brutus; that king of Shakespeare's—Leary, I think you call him—had his own daughters go back on him; Platt had his Odell, and I've got my "The" McManus. It's a real proof that a man is great when he meets with political ingratitude. Great men have a tender, trustin' nature. So have I, outside of the contractin' and real estate business. In politics I have trusted men who have told me they were my friends, and if traitors have turned up in my camp—well, I only had the same experience as Caesar, Leary, and the others. About my Brutus. McManus, you know, has seven brothers and they call him "The" because he is the boss of the lot, and to distinguish him from all other McManuses. For several years he was a political bushwhacker. In campaigns he was sometimes on the fence, sometimes on both sides of the fence, and sometimes under the fence. Nobody knew where to find him at any particular time, and nobody trusted him—that is, nobody but me. I thought there was some good in him after all and that, if I took him in hand, I could make a man of him yet.

I did take him in hand, a few years ago. My friends told me it would be the Brutus-Leary business all over again, but I didn't believe them. I put my trust in "The." I nominated him for the Assembly, and he was elected. A year afterwards, when I was runnin' for re-election as Senator, I nominated him for the Assembly again on the ticket with me. What do you think happened? We both carried the Fifteenth Assembly District, but he ran away ahead of me. Just think! Ahead of me in my own district! I was just dazed. When I began to recover, my election district captains came to me and said that McManus had sold me out with the idea of knockin' me out of the Senatorship, and then tryin' to capture the leadership of the district. I couldn't believe it. My trustin' nature couldn't imagine such treachery.

I sent for McManus and said, with my voice tremblin' with emotions: "They say you have done me dirt, 'The.' It can't be true. Tell me it ain't true."

"The" almost wept as he said he was innocent.

"Never have I done you dirt, George," he declared. "Wicked traitors have tried to do you. I don't know just who they are yet, but I'm on their trail, and I'll find them or abjure the name of 'The' McManus. I'm goin' out right now to find them."

Well, "The" kept his word as far as goin' out and findin' the traitors was concerned. He found them all right—and put himself at their head. Oh, no! He didn't have to go far to look for them. He's got them gathered in his clubrooms now, and he's doin' his best to take the leadership from the man that made him. So you see that Caesar and Leary and me's in the same boat, only I'll come out on top while Caesar and Leary went under.

Now let me tell you that the ingrate in politics never flourishes long. I can give you lots of examples. Look at the men who done up Roscoe Conkling when he resigned from the United States Senate and went to Albany to ask for re-election! What's become of them? Passed from view like a movin' picture. Who took Conkling's place in the Senate? Twenty dollars even that you can't remember his name without looking in the almanac. And poor old Platt! He's down and out now and Odell is in the saddle, but that don't mean that he'll always be in the saddle. His enemies are workin' hard all the time to do him, and I wouldn't be a bit surprised if he went out before the next State campaign.

The politicians who make a lastin' success in politics are the men who are always loyal to their friends, even up to the gate of State prison, if necessary; men who keep their promises and never lie. Richard Croker used to say that tellin' the truth and stickin' to his friends was the political leader's stock in trade. Nobody ever said anything truer, and nobody lived up to it better than Croker. That is why he remained leader of Tammany Hall as long as he wanted to. Every man in the organization trusted him. Sometimes he made mistakes that hurt in campaigns, but they were always on the side of servin' his friends.

It's the same with Charles F. Murphy. He has always stood by his friends even when it looked like he would be downed for doin' so. Remember how he stuck to McClellan in 1903 when all the Brooklyn leaders were against him, and it seemed as if Tammany was in for a grand smash-up! It's men like Croker and Murphy that stay leaders as long as they live; not men like Brutus and McManus.

Now I want to tell you why political traitors, in New York City especially, are punished quick. It's because the Irish are in a majority. The Irish, above all people in the world, hates a traitor. You can't hold them back when a traitor of any kind is in sight and, rememberin' old Ireland, they take particular delight in doin' up a political traitor. Most of the voters in my district are Irish or of Irish descent; they've spotted "The" McManus, and when they get a chance at him at the polls next time, they won't do a thing to him.

The question has been asked: Is a politician ever justified in goin' back on his district leader? I answer: "No; as long as the leader hustles around and gets all the jobs possible for his constituents." When the voters elect a man leader, they make a sort of a contract with him. They say, although it ain't written out: "We've put you here to look out for our interests. You want to see that this district gets all the jobs that's comin' to it. Be faithful to us, and we'll be faithful to you."

The district leader promises and that makes a solemn contract. If he lives up to it, spends most of his time chasin' after places in the departments, picks up jobs from railroads and contractors for his followers, and shows himself in all ways a true statesman, then his followers are bound in honor to uphold him, just as they're bound to uphold the Constitution of the United States. But if he only looks after his own interests or shows no talent for scenting out jobs or ain't got the nerve to demand and get his share of the good things that are goin', his followers may be absolved from their allegiance and they may up and swat him without bein' put down as political ingrates.

Reciprocity in Patronage

WHENEVER Tammany is whipped at the polls, the people set to predictin' that the organization is goin' to smash. They say we can't get along without the offices and that the district leaders are goin' to desert wholesale. That was what was said after the throwdowns in 1894 and 1901. But it didn't happen, did it? Not one big Tammany man deserted, and today the organization is stronger than ever.

How was that? It was because Tammany has more than one string to its bow.

I acknowledge that you can't keep an organization together without patronage. Men ain't in politics for nothin'. They want to get somethin' out of it.

But there is more than one kind of patronage. We lost the public kind, or a greater part of it, in 1901, but Tammany has an immense private patronage that keeps things goin' when it gets a setback at the polls.

Take me, for instance. When Low came in, some of

my men lost public jobs, but I fixed them all right. I don't know how many jobs I got for them on the surface and elevated railroads—several hundred.

I placed a lot more on public works done by contractors, and no Tammany man goes hungry in my district. Plunkitt's O.K. on an application for a job is never turned down, for they all know that Plunkitt and Tammany don't stay out long. See!

Let me tell you, too, that I got jobs from Republicans in office—Federal and otherwise. When Tammany's on top I do good turns for the Republicans. When they're on top they don't forget me.

Me and the Republicans are enemies just one day in the year—election day. Then we fight tooth and nail. The rest of the time it's live and let live with us.

On election day I try to pile up as big a majority as I can against George Wanmaker, the Republican leader of the Fifteenth. Any other day George and I are the best of friends. I can go to him and say: "George, I want you to place this friend of mine." He says: "All right, Senator." Or vice versa.

You see, we differ on tariffs and currencies and all them things, but we agree on the main proposition that when a man works in politics, he should get something out of it.

The politicians have got to stand together this way or there wouldn't be any political parties in a short time. Civil service would gobble up everything, politicians would be on the bum, the republic would fall and soon there would be the cry of "Vevey le roi!"

The very thought of this civil service monster makes my blood boil. I have said a lot about it already, but another instance of its awful work just occurs to me.

Let me tell you a sad but true story. Last Wednesday a line of carriages wound into Cavalry Cemetery. I was in one of them. It was the funeral of a young man from my district—a bright boy that I had great hopes of.

When he went to school, he was the most patriotic boy in the district. Nobody could sing "The Star-Spangled Banner" like him, nobody was as fond of waving a flag, and nobody shot off as many firecrackers on the Fourth of July. And when he grew up he made up his mind to serve his country in one of the city departments. There was no way of gettin' there without passin' a civil service examination. Well, he went down to the civil service office and tackled the fool questions. I saw him next day—it was Memorial Day, and soldiers were marchin' and flags flyin' and people cheerin'.

Where was my young man? Standin' on the corner, scowlin' at the whole show. When I asked him why he was so quiet, he laughed in a wild sort of way and said: "What rot all this is!"

Just then a band came along playing "Liberty." He laughed wild again and said: "Liberty? Rats!"

I don't guess I need to make a long story of it.

From the time that young man left the civil service office he lost all patriotism. He didn't care no more for his country. He went to the dogs.

He ain't the only one. There's a gravestone over some bright young man's head for every one of them infernal civil service examinations. They are underminin' the manhood of the nation and makin' the Declaration of Independence a farce. We need a new Declaration of Independence—independence of the whole fool civil service business.

I mention all this now to show why it is that the politicians of two big parties help each other along, and why Tammany men are tolerably happy when not in power in the city. When we win I won't let any deservin' Republican in my neighborhood suffer from hunger or thirst, although, of course, I look out for my own people first.

Now, I've never gone in for nonpartisan business, but I do think that all the leaders of the two parties should get together and make an open, nonpartisan fight against civil service, their common enemy. They could keep up their quarrels about imperialism and free silver and high tariff. They don't count for much alongside of civil service, which strikes right at the root of the government.

The time is fast coming when civil service or the politicians will have to go. And it will be here sooner than they expect if the politicians don't unite, drop all them minor issues for a while and make a stand against the civil service flood that's sweepin' over the country like them floods out West.

Brooklynites
Natural-Born Hayseeds

SOME people are wonderin' why it is that the Brooklyn Democrats have been sidin' with David B. Hill and the upstate crowd. There's no cause for wonder. I have made a careful study of the Brooklynite, and I can tell you why. It's because a Brooklynite is a natural-born hayseed, and can never become a real New Yorker. He can't be trained into it. Consolidation didn't make him a New Yorker, and nothin' on earth can. A man born in Germany can settle down and become a good New Yorker. So can an Irishman; in fact, the first word an Irish boy learns in the old country is "New York," and when he grows up and comes here, he is at home right away. Even a Jap or a Chinaman can become a New Yorker, but a Brooklynite never can.

And why? Because Brooklyn don't seem to be like any other place on earth. Once let a man grow up amidst Brooklyn's cobblestones, with the odor of

Newton Creek and Gowanus Canal ever in his nostrils, and there's no place in the world for him except Brooklyn. And even if he don't grow up there; if he is born there and lives there only in his boyhood and then moves away, he is still beyond redemption. In one of my speeches in the Legislature, I gave an example of this, and it's worth repeatin' now. Soon after I became a leader on the West Side, a quarter of a century ago, I came across a bright boy, about seven years old, who had just been brought over from Brooklyn by his parents. I took an interest in the boy, and when he grew up I brought him into politics. Finally, I sent him to the Assembly from my district. Now remember that the boy was only seven years old when he left Brooklyn, and was twenty-three when he went to the Assembly. You'd think he had forgotten all about Brooklyn, wouldn't you? I did, but I was dead wrong. When that young fellow got into the Assembly he paid no attention to bills or debates about New York City. He didn't even show any interest in his own district. But just let Brooklyn be mentioned, or a bill be introduced about Gowanus Canal, or the Long Island Railroad, and he was all attention. Nothin' else on earth interested him.

The end came when I caught him—what do you think I caught him at? One mornin' I went over from the Senate to the Assembly chamber, and there I found my young man readin'—actually readin' a Brooklyn newspaper! When he saw me comin' he tried to hide the paper, but it was too late. I caught him dead to rights, and I said to him: "Jimmy, I'm afraid New York ain't fascinatin' enough for you. You had better move back to Brooklyn after your present term." And he did. I met him the other day crossin' the Brooklyn Bridge, carryin' a hobbyhorse under one arm, and a doll's carriage under the other, and lookin' perfectly happy.

McCarren and his men are the same way. They can't get it into their heads that they are New Yorkers, and just tend naturally toward supportin' Hill and his hayseeds against Murphy. I had some hopes of McCarren till lately. He spends so much of his time over here and has seen so much of the world that I thought he might be an exception, and grow out of his Brooklyn surroundings, but his course at Albany shows that there is no exception to the rule. Say, I'd rather take a Hottentot in hand to bring up as a good New Yorker than undertake the job with a Brooklynite. Honest, I would.

And, by the way, come to think of it, is there really any upstate Democrats left? It has never been proved to my satisfaction that there is any. I know that some upstate members of the State committee call themselves Democrats. Besides these, I know at least six more men above the Bronx who make a livin' out of professin' to be Democrats, and I have just heard of some few more. But if there is any real Democrats up the State, what becomes of them on election day? They certainly don't go near the polls or they vote the Republican ticket. Look at the last three State elections! Roosevelt piled up more than 100,000 majority above the Bronx; Odell piled up about 160,000 majority the first time he ran and 131,000 the second time. About all the Democratic votes cast were polled in New York City. The Republicans can get all the votes they want up the State. Even when we piled up

123,000 majority for Coler in the city in 1902, the Republicans went it 8000 better above the Bronx.

That's why it makes me mad to hear about upstate Democrats controllin' our State convention, and sayin' who we shall choose for President. It's just like Staten Island undertakin' to dictate to a New York City convention. I remember once a Syracuse man came to Richard Croker at the Democratic Club, handed him a letter of introduction and said: "I'm lookin' for a job in the Street Cleanin' Department; I'm backed by a hundred upstate Democrats." Croker looked hard at the man a minute and then said: "Upstate Democrats! Upstate Democrats! I didn't know there was any upstate Democrats. Just walk up and down a while till I see what an upstate Democrat looks like."

Another thing. When a campaign is on, did you ever hear of an upstate Democrat makin' a contribution? Not much. Tammany has had to foot the whole bill, and when any of Hill's men came down to New York to help him in the campaign, we had to pay their board. Whenever money is to be raised, there's nothin' doin' up the State. The Democrats there— always providin' that there is any Democrats there— take to the woods. Supposin' Tammany turned over the campaigns to the Hill men and then held off, what would happen? Why, they would have to hire a shed out in the suburbs of Albany for a headquarters, unless the Democratic National Committee put up for the campaign expenses. Tammany's got the votes and the cash. The Hill crowd's only got hot air.

Tammany Leaders
Not Bookworms

You hear a lot of talk about the Tammany district leaders bein' illiterate men. If illiterate means havin' common sense, we plead guilty. But if they mean that the Tammany leaders ain't got no education and ain't gents they don't know what they're talkin' about. Of course, we ain't all bookworms and college professors. If we were, Tammany might win an election one in four thousand years. Most of the leaders are plain American citizens, of the people and near to the people, and they have all the education they need to whip the dudes who part their name in the middle and to run the City Government. We've got bookworms, too, in the organization. But we don't make them district leaders. We keep them for ornaments on parade days.

Tammany Hall is a great big machine, with every part adjusted delicate to do its own particular work. It runs so smooth that you wouldn't think it was a complicated affair, but it is. Every district leader is fitted to the district he runs and he wouldn't exactly fit any other district. That's the reason Tammany never makes the mistake the Fusion outfit always makes of sendin' men into the districts who don't know the people, and have no sympathy with their peculiarities. We don't put a silk stockin' on the Bowery, nor do we make a man who is handy with his fists leader of the Twenty-ninth. The Fusionists make about the same sort of a mistake that a repeater made at an election in Albany several years ago. He was hired to go to the polls early in a half-dozen election districts and vote on other men's names before these men reached the polls. At one place, when he was asked his name by the poll clerk, he had the nerve to answer "William Croswell Doane."

"Come off. You ain't Bishop Doane," said the poll clerk.

"The hell I ain't, you ————!" yelled the repeater.

Now, that is the sort of bad judgment the Fusionists are guilty of. They don't pick men to suit the work they have to do.

Take me, for instance. My district, the Fifteenth, is made up of all sorts of people, and a cosmopolitan is needed to run it successful. I'm a cosmopolitan. When I get into the silk-stockin' part of the district, I can talk grammar and all that with the best of them. I went to school three winters when I was a boy, and I learned a lot of fancy stuff that I keep for occasions. There ain't a silk stockin' in the district who ain't proud to be seen talkin' with George Washington Plunkitt, and maybe they learn a thing or two from their talks with me. There's one man in the district, a big banker, who said to me one day: "George, you can sling the most vigorous English I ever heard. You remind me of Senator Hoar of Massachusetts." Of course, that was puttin' it on too thick; but say, honest, I like Senator Hoar's speeches. He once quoted in the United States Senate some of my remarks on the curse of civil service, and, though he didn't agree with me altogether, I noticed that our ideas are alike in some things, and we both have the knack of puttin' things strong, only he put on more frills to suit his audience.

As for the common people of the district, I am at home with them at all times. When I go among them, I don't try to show off my grammar, or talk about the Constitution, or how many volts there is in electricity or make it appear in any way that I am better educated than they are. They wouldn't stand for that sort of thing. No; I drop all monkeyshines. So you see, I've got to be several sorts of a man in a single day, a lightnin' change artist, so to speak. But I am one sort of man always in one respect: I stick to my friends high and low, do them a good turn whenever I get a chance, and hunt up all the jobs going for my constituents. There ain't a man in New York who's got such a scent for political jobs as I have. When I get up in the mornin' I can almost tell every time whether a job has become vacant over night, and what department it's in and I'm the first man on the ground to get it. Only last week I turned up at the office of Water Register Savage at 9 A.M. and told him I wanted a vacant place in his office for one of my constituents. "How did you know that O'Brien had got out?" he asked me. "I smelled it in the air when I got up this

mornin'," I answered. Now, that was the fact. I
didn't know there was a man in the department
named O'Brien, much less that he had got out, but
my scent led me to the Water Register's office, and it
don't often lead me wrong.

A cosmopolitan ain't needed in all the other districts, but our men are just the kind to rule. There's
Dan Finn, in the Battery district, bluff, jolly Dan, who
is now on the bench. Maybe you'd think that a court
justice is not the man to hold a district like that, but
you're mistaken. Most of the voters of the district are
the janitors of the big office buildings on lower Broadway and their helpers. These janitors are the most
dignified and haughtiest of men. Even I would have
trouble in holding them. Nothin' less than a judge on
the bench is good enough for them. Dan does the
dignity act with the janitors, and when he is with the
boys he hangs up the ermine in the closet and becomes a jolly good fellow.

Big Tom Foley, leader of the Second District, fits in
exactly, too. Tom sells whisky, and good whisky, and
he is able to take care of himself against a half dozen
thugs if he runs up against them on Cherry Hill or in
Chatham Square. Pat Ryder and Johnnie Ahearn of
the Third and Fourth Districts are just the men for
the places. Ahearn's constituents are about half Irishmen and half Jews. He is as popular with one race as
with the other. He eats corned beef and kosher meat
with equal nonchalance, and it's all the same to him
whether he takes off his hat in the church or pulls it
down over his ears in the synagogue.

The other downtown leaders, Barney Martin of the
Fifth, Tim Sullivan of the Sixth, Pat Keahon of the

Seventh, Florrie Sullivan of the Eighth, Frank Goodwin of the Ninth, Julius Harburger of the Tenth, Pete Dooling of the Eleventh, Joe Scully of the Twelfth, Johnnie Oakley of the Fourteenth, and Pat Keenan of the Sixteenth are just built to suit the people they have to deal with. They don't go in for literary business much downtown, but these men are all real gents, and that's what the people want—even the poorest tenement dwellers. As you go farther uptown you find a rather different kind of district leader. There's Victor Dowling who was until lately the leader of the Twenty-fourth. He's a lulu. He knows the Latin grammar backward. What's strange, he's a sensible young fellow, too. About once in a century we come across a fellow like that in Tammany politics. James J. Martin, leader of the Twenty-seventh, is also something of a hightoner, and publishes a law paper, while Thomas E. Rush, of the Twenty-ninth, is a lawyer, and Isaac Hopper, of the Thirty-first, is a big contractor. The downtown leaders wouldn't do uptown, and vice versa. So, you see, these fool critics don't know what they're talkin' about when they criticize Tammany Hall, the most perfect political machine on earth.

Dangers of the Dress Suit
in Politics

PUTTIN' on style don't pay in politics. The people won't stand for it. If you've got an achin' for style, sit down on it till you have made your pile and landed a Supreme Court Justiceship with a fourteen-year term at $17,500 a year, or some job of that kind. Then you've got about all you can get out of politics, and you can afford to wear a dress suit all day and sleep in it all night if you have a mind to. But, before you have caught onto your life meal ticket, be simple. Live like your neighbors even if you have the means to live better. Make the poorest man in your district feel that he is your equal, or even a bit superior to you.

Above all things, avoid a dress suit. You have no idea of the harm that dress suits have done in politics. They are not so fatal to young politicians as civil service reform and drink, but they have scores of victims. I will mention one sad case. After the big Tammany victory in 1897, Richard Croker went down to Lakewood to make up the slate of offices for Mayor Van Wyck to distribute. All the district leaders and many more Tammany men went down there, too, to pick up anything good that was goin'. There was nothin' but dress suits at dinner at Lakewood, and Croker wouldn't let any Tammany men go to dinner without them. Well, a bright young West Side politician, who held a three-thousand-dollar job in one of the departments, went to Lakewood to ask Croker for something better. He wore a dress suit for the first time in his life. It was his undoin'. He got stuck on himself. He thought he looked too beautiful for anything, and when he came home he was a changed man. As soon as he got to his house every evenin' he put on that dress suit and set around in it until bedtime. That didn't satisfy him long. He wanted others to see how beautiful he was in a dress suit; so he joined dancin' clubs and began goin' to all the balls that was given in town. Soon he began to neglect his family. Then he took to drinkin', and didn't pay any attention to his political work in the district. The end came in less than a year. He was dismissed from the department and went to the dogs. The other day I met him rigged out almost like a hobo, but he still had a dress-suit vest on. When I asked him what he was doin', he said: "Nothin' at present, but I got a promise of a job enrollin' voters at Citizens' Union headquarters." Yes, a dress suit had brought him that low!

I'll tell you another case right in my own Assembly District. A few years ago I had as one of my lieutenants a man named Zeke Thompson. He did fine work for me and I thought he had a bright future. One day he came to me, said he intended to buy an option on a house, and asked me to help him out. I like to see a young man acquirin' property and I had so much confidence in Zeke that I put up for him on the house.

A month or so afterwards I heard strange rumors. People told me that Zeke was beginnin' to put on style. They said he had a billiard table in his house and had hired Jap servants. I couldn't believe it. The idea of a Democrat, a follower of George Washington Plunkitt in the Fifteenth Assembly District havin' a billiard table and Jap servants! One mornin' I called at the house to give Zeke a chance to clear himself. A Jap opened the door for me. I saw the billiard table. Zeke was guilty! When I got over the shock, I said to Zeke: "You are caught with the goods on. No excuses will go. The Democrats of this district ain't used to dukes and princes and we wouldn't feel comfortable in your company. You'd overpower us. You had better move up to the Nineteenth or Twenty-seventh District, and hang a silk stocking on your door." He went up to the Nineteenth, turned Republican, and was lookin' for an Albany job the last I heard of him.

Now, nobody ever saw me puttin' on any style. I'm the same Plunkitt I was when I entered politics forty years ago. That is why the people of the district have confidence in me. If I went into the stylish business, even I, Plunkitt, might be thrown down in the district. That was shown pretty clearly in the senatorial fight last year. A day before the election, my enemies circulated a report that I had ordered a $10,000 automobile and a $125 dress suit. I sent out contradictions as fast as I could, but I wasn't able to stamp out the infamous slander before the votin' was over, and I suffered some at the polls. The people wouldn't have minded much if I had been accused of robbin' the city treasury, for they're used to slanders of that kind in campaigns, but the automobile and the dress suit were too much for them.

Another thing that people won't stand for is showin' off your learnin'. That's just puttin' on style in another way. If you're makin' speeches in a campaign, talk the language the people talk. Don't try to show how the situation is by quotin' Shakespeare. Shakespeare was all right in his way, but he didn't know anything about Fifteenth District politics. If you know Latin and Greek and have a hankerin' to work them off on somebody, hire a stranger to come to your house and listen to you for a couple of hours; then go out and talk the language of the Fifteenth to the people. I know it's an awful temptation, the hankerin' to show off your learnin'. I've felt it myself, but I always resist it. I know the awful consequences.

On Municipal Ownership

I AM for municipal ownership on one condition: that the civil service law be repealed. It's a grand idea— the city ownin' the railroads, the gas works and all that. Just see how many thousands of new places there would be for the workers in Tammany! Why, there would be almost enough to go around, if no civil service law stood in the way. My plan is this: first get rid of that infamous law, and then go ahead and by degrees get municipal ownership.

Some of the reformers are sayin' that municipal ownership won't do because it would give a lot of patronage to the politicians. How those fellows mix things up when they argue! They're givin' the strongest argument in favor of municipal ownership when they say that. Who is better fitted to run the railroads and the gas plants and the ferries than the men who make a business of lookin' after the interests of the city? Who is more anxious to serve the city? Who needs the jobs more?

Look at the Dock Department! The city owns the docks, and how beautiful Tammany manages them! I can't tell you how many places they provide for our workers. I know there is a lot of talk about dock graft, but that talk comes from the outs. When the Republicans had the docks under Low and Strong, you didn't hear them sayin' anything about graft, did you? No; they just went in and made hay while the sun shone. That's always the case. When the reformers are out they raise the yell that Tammany men should be sent to jail. When they get in, they're so busy keepin' out of jail themselves that they don't have no time to attack Tammany.

All I want is that municipal ownership be postponed till I get my bill repealin' the civil service law before the next legislature. It would be all a mess if every man who wanted a job would have to run up against a civil service examination. For instance, if a man wanted a job as motorman on a surface car, it's ten to one that they would ask him: "Who wrote the Latin grammar, and, if so, why did he write it? How many years were you at college? Is there any part of the Greek language you don't know? State all you don't know, and why you don't know it. Give a list of all the sciences with full particulars about each one and how it came to be discovered. Write out word for word the last ten decisions of the United States Supreme Court and show if they conflict with the last ten decisions of the police courts of New York City."

Before the would-be motorman left the civil service room, the chances are he would be a raving lunatic.

Anyhow I wouldn't like to ride on his car. Just here I want to say one last final word about civil service. In the last ten years I have made an investigation which I've kept quiet till this time. Now I have all the figures together, and I'm ready to announce the result. My investigation was to find out how many civil service reformers and how many politicians were in state prisons. I discovered that there was forty per cent more civil service reformers among the jailbirds. If any legislative committee wants the detailed figures, I'll prove what I say. I don't want to give the figures now, because I want to keep them to back me up when I go to Albany to get the civil service law repealed. Don't you think that when I've had my inning, the civil service law will go down, and the people will see that the politicians are all right, and that they ought to have the job of runnin' things when municipal ownership comes?

One thing more about municipal ownership. If the city owned the railroads, etc., salaries would be sure to go up. Higher salaries is the cryin' need of the day. Municipal ownership would increase them all along the line and would stir up such patriotism as New York City never knew before. You can't be patriotic on a salary that just keeps the wolf from the door. Any man who pretends he can will bear watchin'. Keep your hand on your watch and pocketbook when he's about. But, when a man has a good fat salary, he finds himself hummin' "Hail Columbia," all unconscious and he fancies, when he's ridin' in a trolley car, that the wheels are always sayin': "Yankee Doodle Came to Town." I know how it is myself. When I got my first good job from the city I bought up all the firecrackers in my district to salute this glorious country. I couldn't wait for the Fourth of July. I got the boys on the block to fire them off for me, and I felt proud of bein' an American. For a long time after that I use to wake up nights singin' "The Star-Spangled Banner."

Tammany the Only Lastin' Democracy

I'VE seen more than one hundred "Democracies" rise and fall in New York City in the last quarter of a century. At least a half-dozen new so-called Democratic organizations are formed every year. All of them go in to down Tammany and take its place, but they seldom last more than a year or two, while Tammany's like the everlastin' rocks, the eternal hills and the blockades on the "L" road—it goes on forever.

I recall offhand the County Democracy, which was the only real opponent Tammany has had in my time, the Irving Hall Democracy, the New York State Democracy, the German-American Democracy, the Protection Democracy, the Independent County Democracy, the Greater New York Democracy, the Jimmy O'Brien Democracy, the Delicatessen Dealers' Democracy, the Silver Democracy, and the Italian Democracy. Not one of them is livin' today, although I hear somethin' about the ghost of the Greater New

York Democracy bein' seen on Broadway once or twice a year.

In the old days of the County Democracy, a new Democratic organization meant some trouble for Tammany—for a time anyhow. Nowadays a new Democracy means nothin' at all except that about a dozen bone-hunters have got together for one campaign only to try to induce Tammany to give them a job or two, or in order to get in with the reformers for the same purpose. You might think that it would cost a lot of money to get up one of these organizations and keep it goin' for even one campaign, but, Lord bless you! it costs next to nothin'. Jimmy O'Brien brought the manufacture of "Democracies" down to an exact science, and reduced the cost of production so as to bring it within the reach of all. Any man with $50 can now have a "Democracy" of his own.

I've looked into the industry, and can give rock-bottom figures. Here's the items of cost of a new "Democracy":

A dinner to twelve bone-hunters	$12.00
A speech on Jeffersonian Democracy	00.00
A proclamation of principles (typewriting)	2.00
Rent of a small room one month for headquarters	12.00
Stationery	2.00
Twelve secondhand chairs	6.00
One secondhand table	2.00
Twenty-nine cuspidors	9.00
Sign painting	5.00
Total	$50.00

Is there any reason for wonder, then, that "Democracies" spring up all over when a municipal campaign is comin' on? If you land even one small job, you get a big return on your investment. You don't have to pay for advertisin' in the papers. The New York papers tumble over one another to give columns to any new organization that comes out against Tammany. In describin' the formation of a "Democracy" on the $50 basis, accordin' to the items I give, the papers would say somethin' like this: "The organization of the Delicatessen Democracy last night threatens the existence of Tammany Hall. It is a grand move for a new and pure Democracy in this city. Well may the Tammany leaders be alarmed; panic has already broke loose in Fourteenth Street. The vast crowd that gathered at the launching of the new organization, the stirrin' speeches and the proclamation of principles mean that, at last, there is an uprisin' that will end Tammany's career of corruption. The Delicatessen Democracy will open in a few days spacious headquarters where all true Democrats may gather and prepare for the fight."

Say, ain't some of the papers awful gullible about politics? Talk about come-ons from Iowa or Texas— they ain't in it with the childlike simplicity of these papers.

It's a wonder to me that more men don't go into this kind of manufacturin' industry. It has bigger profits generally than the green-goods business and none of the risks. And you don't have to invest as much as the green-goods men. Just see what good things some of these "Democracies" got in the last few years! The New York State Democracy in 1897 landed a Supreme Court Justiceship for the man who manufactured the concern—a fourteen-year term at $17,500 a year, that is $245,000. You see, Tammany was rather scared that year and was bluffed into givin' this job to get the support of the State Democracy which, by the way, went out of business quick and prompt the day after it got this big plum. The next year the German Democracy landed a place of the same kind. And then see how the Greater New York Democracy worked the game on the reformers in 1901! The men who managed this concern were former Tammanyites who had lost their grip; yet they made the Citizens' Union innocents believe that they were the real thing in the way of reformers, and that they had 100,000 votes back of them. They got the Borough President of Manhattan, the President of the Board of Aldermen, the Register and a lot of lesser places. It was the greatest bunco game of modern times.

And then, in 1894, when Strong was elected mayor, what a harvest it was for all the little "Democracies" that was made to order that year! Every one of them got somethin' good. In one case, all the nine men in an organization got jobs payin' from $2000 to $5000. I happen to know exactly what it cost to manufacture that organization. It was $42.04. They left out the stationery, and had only twenty-three cuspidors. The extra four cents was for two postage stamps.

The only reason I can imagine why more men don't go into this industry is because they don't know about it. And just here it strikes me that it might not be wise to publish what I've said. Perhaps if it gets to be known what a snap this manufacture of "Democracies" is, all the green-goods men, the bunco-steerers, and the young Napoleons of finance will go into it and the public will be humbugged more than it has been. But, after all, what difference would it make? There's always a certain number of suckers and a certain number of men lookin' for a chance to take them in, and the suckers are sure to be took one way or another. It's the everlastin' law of demand and supply.

Concerning Gas in Politics

SINCE the eighty-cent gas bill was defeated in Albany, everybody's talkin' about senators bein' bribed. Now, I wasn't in the Senate last session, and I don't know the ins and outs of everything that was done, but I can tell you that the legislators are often hauled over the coals when they are all on the level. I've been there and I know. For instance, when I voted in the Senate in 1904, for the Remsen Bill that the newspapers called the "Astoria Gas Grab Bill," they didn't do a thing to me. The papers kept up a howl about all the supporters of the bill bein' bought up by the Consolidated Gas Company, and the Citizens' Union did me the honor to call me the commander-in-chief of the "Black Horse Cavalry."

The fact is that I was workin' for my district all this time, and I wasn't bribed by nobody. There's several of these gashouses in the district, and I wanted to get them over to Astoria for three reasons: first, because they're nuisances; second, because there's no votes in them for me any longer; third, because—well, I had a little private reason which I'll explain further on. I needn't explain how they're nuisances. They're worse than open sewers. Still, I might have stood that if they hadn't degenerated so much in the last few years.

Ah, gashouses ain't what they used to be! Not very long ago, each gashouse was good for a couple of hundred votes. All the men employed in them were Irishmen and Germans who lived in the district. Now, it is all different. The men are dagoes who live across in Jersey and take no interest in the district. What's the use of havin' ill-smellin' gashouses if there's no votes in them?

Now, as to my private reason. Well, I'm a business man and go in for any business that's profitable and honest. Real estate is one of my specialties. I know the value of every foot of ground in my district, and I calculated long ago that if them gashouses was removed, surroundin' property would go up 100 per cent. When the Remsen Bill, providin' for the removal of the gashouses to Queens County came up, I said to myself: "George, hasn't your chance come?" I answered: "Sure." Then I sized up the chances of the bill. I found it was certain to pass the Senate and the Assembly, and I got assurances straight from headquarters that Governor Odell would sign it. Next I came down to the city to find out the mayor's position. I got it straight that he would approve the bill, too.

Can't you guess what I did then? Like any sane man who had my information, I went in and got options on a lot of the property around the gashouses.

Well, the bill went through the Senate and the Assembly all right and the mayor signed it, but Odell backslided at the last minute and the whole game fell through. If it had succeeded, I guess I would have been accused of graftin'. What I want to know is, what do you call it when I got left and lost a pot of money?

I not only lost money, but I was abused for votin' for the bill. Wasn't that outrageous? They said I was in with the Consolidated Gas Company and all other kinds of rot, when I was really only workin' for my district and tryin' to turn an honest penny on the side. Anyhow I got a little fun out of the business. When the Remsen Bill was up, I was tryin' to put through a bill of my own, the Spuyten Duyvil Bill, which provided for fillin' in some land under water that the New York Central Railroad wanted. Well, the Remsen managers were afraid of bein' beaten and they went around offerin' to make trades with senators and assemblymen who had bills they were anxious to pass. They came to me and offered six votes for my Spuyten Duyvil Bill in exchange for my vote on the Remsen Bill. I took them up in a hurry, and they felt pretty sore afterwards when they heard I was goin' to vote for the Remsen Bill anyhow.

A word about that Spuyten Duyvil Bill—I was criticized a lot for introducin' it. They said I was workin' in the interest of the New York Central, and was goin' to get the contract for fillin' in. The fact is, that the fillin' in was a good thing for the city, and if it helped the New York Central, too, what of it? The railroad is a great public institution, and I was never an enemy of public institutions. As to the contract, it hasn't come along yet. If it does come, it will find me at home at all proper and reasonable hours, if there is a good profit in sight.

The papers and some people are always ready to find wrong motives in what us statesmen do. If we bring about some big improvement that benefits the city and it just happens, as a sort of coincidence, that we make a few dollars out of the improvement, they say we are grafters. But we are used to this kind of ingratitude. It falls to the lot of all statesmen, especially Tammany statesmen. All we can do is to bow our heads in silence and wait till time has cleared our memories.

Just think of mentionin' dishonest graft in connection with the name of George Washington Plunkitt, the man who gave the city its magnificent chain of parks, its Washington Bridge, its Speedway, its Museum of Natural History, its One Hundred and Fifty-fifth Street Viaduct and its West Side Courthouse! I was the father of the bills that provided for all these; yet, because I supported the Remsen and Spuyten Duyvil bills, some people have questioned my honest motives. If that's the case, how can you expect legislators to fare who are not the fathers of the parks, the Washington Bridge, the Speedway and the Viaduct?

Now, understand; I ain't defendin' the senators who killed the eighty-cent gas bill. I don't know why they acted as they did; I only want to impress the idea to go slow before you make up your mind that a man, occupyin' the exalted position that I held for so many years, has done wrong. For all I know, these senators may have been as honest and high-minded about the gas bill as I was about the Remsen and Spuyten Duyvil bills.

Plunkitt's Fondest Dream

THE time is comin' and though I'm no youngster, I may see it, when New York City will break away from the State and become a state itself. It's got to come. The feelin' between this city and the hayseeds that make a livin' by plunderin' it is every bit as bitter as the feelin' between the North and South before the war. And, let me tell you, if there ain't a peaceful separation before long, we may have the horrors of civil war right here in New York State. Why, I know a lot of men in my district who would like nothin' better today than to go out gunnin' for hayseeds!

New York City has got a bigger population than most of the states in the Union. It's got more wealth than any dozen of them. Yet the people here, as I explained before, are nothin' but slaves of the Albany gang. We have stood the slavery a long, long time, but the uprisin' is near at hand. It will be a fight for liberty, just like the American Revolution. We'll get liberty peacefully if we can; by cruel war if we must.

Just think how lovely things would be here if we had a Tammany Governor and Legislature meetin', say in the neighborhood of Fifty-ninth Street, and a Tammany Mayor and Board of Aldermen doin' business in City Hall! How sweet and peaceful everything would go on! The people wouldn't have to bother about nothin'. Tammany would take care of everything for them in its nice quiet way. You wouldn't hear of any conflicts between the state and city authorities. They would settle everything pleasant and comfortable at Tammany Hall, and every bill introduced in the Legislature by Tammany would be sure to go through. The Republicans wouldn't count.

Imagine how the city would be built up in a short time! At present we can't make a public improvement of any consequence without goin' to Albany for permission, and most of the time we get turned down when we go there. But, with a Tammany Governor and Legislature up at Fifty-ninth Street, how public works would hum here! The Mayor and Aldermen could decide on an improvement, telephone the Capitol, have a bill put through in a jiffy and—there you are. We could have a state constitution, too, which would extend the debt limit so that we could issue a whole lot more bonds. As things are now, all the money spent for docks, for instance, is charged against the city in calculatin' the debt limit, although the Dock Department provides immense revenues. It's the same with some other departments. This humbug would be dropped if Tammany ruled at the

Capitol and the City Hall, and the city would have money to burn.

Another thing—the constitution of the new state wouldn't have a word about civil service, and if any man dared to introduce any kind of a civil service bill in the Legislature, he would be fired out the window. Then we would have government of the people by the people who were elected to govern them. That's the kind of government Lincoln meant. O what a glorious future for the city! Whenever I think of it I feel like goin' out and celebratin', and I'm really almost sorry that I don't drink.

You may ask what would become of the upstate people if New York City left them in the lurch and went into the State business on its own account. Well, we wouldn't be under no obligation to provide for them; still I would be in favor of helpin' them along for a while until they could learn to work and earn an honest livin', just like the United States Government looks after the Indians. These hayseeds have been so used to livin' off of New York City that they would be helpless after we left them. It wouldn't do to let them starve. We might make some sort of an appropriation for them for a few years, but it would be with the distinct understandin' that they must get busy right away and learn to support themselves. If, after say five years, they weren't self-supportin', we could withdraw the appropriation and let them shift for themselves. The plan might succeed and it might not. We'd be doin' our duty anyhow.

Some persons might say: "But how about it if the hayseed politicians moved down here and went in to get control of the government of the new state?" We could provide against that easy by passin' a law that these politicians couldn't come below the Bronx without a sort of passport limitin' the time of their stay here, and forbiddin' them to monkey with politics here. I don't know just what kind of a bill would be required to fix this, but with a Tammany Constitution, Governor, Legislature and Mayor, there would be no trouble in settlin' a little matter of that sort.

Say, I don't wish I was a poet, for if I was, I guess I'd be livin' in a garret on no dollars a week instead of runnin' a great contractin' and transportation business which is doin' pretty well, thank you; but, honest, now, the notion takes me sometimes to yell poetry of the red-hot-hail-glorious-land kind when I think of New York City as a state by itself.

Tammany's Patriotism

TAMMANY'S the most patriotic organization on earth, notwithstandin' the fact that the civil service law is sappin' the foundations of patriotism all over the country. Nobody pays any attention to the Fourth of July any longer except Tammany and the small boy. When the Fourth comes, the reformers, with Revolutionary names parted in the middle, run off to Newport or the Adirondacks to get out of the way of the noise and everything that reminds them of the glorious day. How different it is with Tammany! The very constitution of the Tammany Society requires that we must assemble at the wigwam on the Fourth, regardless of the weather, and listen to the readin' of the Declaration of Independence and patriotic speeches.

You ought to attend one of these meetin's. They're a liberal education in patriotism. The great hall upstairs is filled with five thousand people, suffocatin' from heat and smoke. Every man Jack of these five thousand knows that down in the basement there's a hundred cases of champagne and two hundred kegs of beer ready to flow when the signal is given. Yet that crowd stick to their seats without turnin' a hair while, for four solid hours, the Declaration of Independence is read, long-winded orators speak, and the glee club sings itself hoarse.

Talk about heroism in the battlefield! That comes and passes away in a moment. You ain't got time to be anything but heroic. But just think of five thousand men sittin' in the hottest place on earth for four long hours, with parched lips and gnawin' stomachs, and knowin' all the time that the delights of the oasis in the desert were only two flights downstairs! Ah, that is the highest kind of patriotism, the patriotism of long sufferin' and endurance. What man wouldn't rather face a cannon for a minute or two than thirst for four hours, with champagne and beer almost under his nose?

And then see how they applaud and yell when patriotic things are said! As soon as the man on the platform starts off with "when, in the course of human events," word goes around that it's the Declaration of Independence, and a mighty roar goes up. The Declaration ain't a very short document and the crowd has heard it on every Fourth but they give it just as fine a send-off as if it was brand-new and awful excitin'. Then the "long talkers" get in their work, that is two or three orators who are good for an hour each. Heat never has any effect on these men. They use every minute of their time. Sometimes human nature gets the better of a man in the audience and he begins to nod, but he always wakes up with a hurrah for the Declaration of Independence.

The greatest hero of the occasion is the Grand Sachem of the Tammany Society who presides. He and the rest of us Sachems come on the stage wearin' stovepipe hats, accordin' to the constitution, but we can shed ours right off, while the Grand Sachem is required to wear his hat all through the celebration. Have you any idea what that means? Four hours under a big silk hat in a hall where the heat registers 110 and the smoke 250! And the Grand Sachem is expected to look pleasant all the time and say nice things when introducin' the speakers! Often his hand goes to his hat, unconscious-like, then he catches himself up in time and looks around like a man who is in the tenth story of a burnin' buildin' seekin' a way to escape. I believe that Fourth-of-July silk hat shortened the life of one of our Grand Sachems, the late Supreme Court Justice Smyth, and I know that one of our Sachems refused the office of Grand Sachem because he couldn't get up sufficient patriotism to perform this four-hour hat act. You see, there's degrees of patriotism just as there's degrees in everything else.

You don't hear of the Citizens' Union people holdin' Fourth-of-July celebrations under a five-pound silk hat, or any other way, do you? The Cits take the Fourth like a dog I had when I was a boy. That dog knew as much as some Cits and he acted just like them about the glorious day. Exactly forty-eight hours before each Fourth of July, the dog left our house on a run and hid himself in the Bronx woods. The day after the Fourth he turned up at home as regular as clockwork. He must have known what a dog is up against on the Fourth. Anyhow, he kept out of the way. The name-parted-in-the-middle aristocrats act in just the same way. They don't want to be annoyed with firecrackers and the Declaration of Independence, and when they see the Fourth comin' they hustle off to the woods like my dog.

Tammany don't only show its patriotism at Fourth-of-July celebrations. It's always on deck when the country needs its services. After the Spanish-American War broke out, John J. Scannell, the Tammany leader of the Twenty-fifth District, wrote to Governor Black offerin' to raise a Tammany regiment to go to the front. If you want proof, go to Tammany Hall and see the beautiful set of engrossed resolutions about this regiment. It's true that the Governor didn't accept the offer, but it showed Tammany's patriotism. Some enemies of the organization have said that the offer to raise the regiment was made after the Governor let it be known that no more volunteers were wanted, but that's the talk of envious slanderers.

Now, a word about Tammany's love for the American flag. Did you ever see Tammany Hall decorated for a celebration? It's just a mass of flags. They even take down the window shades and put flags in place of them. There's flags everywhere except on the floors. We don't care for expense where the American flag is concerned, especially after we have won an election. In 1904 we originated the custom of givin' a small flag to each man as he entered Tammany Hall for the Fourth-of-July celebration. It took like wildfire. The men waved their flags whenever they cheered and the sight made me feel so patriotic that I forgot all about civil service for a while. And the good work of the flags didn't stop there. The men carried them home and gave them to the children, and the kids got patriotic, too. Of course, it all cost a pretty penny, but what of that? We had won at the polls the precedin' November, had the offices and could afford to make an extra investment in patriotism.

On the Use of Money
in Politics

THE civil service gang is always howlin' about candidates and officeholders puttin' up money for campaigns and about corporations chippin' in. They might as well howl about givin' contributions to churches. A political organization has to have money for its business as well as a church, and who has more right to put up than the men who get the good things that are goin'? Take, for instance, a great political concern like Tammany Hall. It does missionary work like a church, it's got big expenses and it's got to be supported by the faithful. If a corporation sends in a check to help the good work of the Tammany Society, why shouldn't we take it like other missionary societies? Of course, the day may come when we'll reject the money of the rich as tainted, but it hadn't come when I left Tammany Hall at 11:25 A.M. today.

Not long ago some newspapers had fits because the Assemblyman from my district said he had put up $500 when he was nominated for the Assembly last year. Every politician in town laughed at these papers. I don't think there was even a Citizens' Union man who didn't know that candidates of both parties have to chip in for campaign expenses. The sums they pay are accordin' to their salaries and the length of their terms of office, if elected. Even candidates for the Supreme Court have to fall in line. A Supreme Court Judge in New York County gets $17,500 a year, and he's expected, when nominated, to help along the good cause with a year's salary. Why not? He has fourteen years on the bench ahead of him, and ten thousand other lawyers would be willin' to put up twice as much to be in his shoes. Now, I ain't sayin' that we sell nominations. That's a different thing altogether. There's no auction and no regular biddin'. The man is picked out and somehow he gets to understand what's expected of him in the way of a contribution, and he ponies up—all from gratitude to the organization that honored him, see?

Let me tell you an instance that shows the difference between sellin' nominations and arrangin' them in the way I described. A few years ago a Republican district leader controlled the nomination for Congress in his Congressional district. Four men wanted it. At first the leader asked for bids privately, but decided at last that the best thing to do was to get the four men together in the back room of a certain saloon and have an open auction. When he had his men lined up, he got on a chair, told about the value of the goods for sale, and asked for bids in regular auctioneer style. The highest bidder got the nomination for

$5000. Now, that wasn't right at all. These things ought to be always fixed up nice and quiet.

As to officeholders, they would be ingrates if they didn't contribute to the organization that put them in office. They needn't be assessed. That would be against the law. But they know what's expected of them, and if they happen to forget they can be reminded polite and courteous. Dan Donegan, who used to be the Wiskinkie of the Tammany Society, and received contributions from grateful officeholders, had a pleasant way of remindin'. If a man forgot his duty to the organization that made him, Dan would call on the man, smile as sweet as you please and say: "You haven't been round at the Hall lately, have you?" If the man tried to slide around the question, Dan would say: "It's gettin' awful cold." Then he would have a fit of shiverin' and walk away. What could be more polite and, at the same time, more to the point? No force, no threats—only a little shiverin' which any man is liable to even in summer.

Just here, I want to charge one more crime to the infamous civil service law. It has made men turn ungrateful. A dozen years ago, when there wasn't much civil service business in the city government, and when the administration could turn out almost any man holdin' office, Dan's shiver took effect every time and there was no ingratitude in the city departments. But when the civil service law came in and all the clerks got lead-pipe cinches on their jobs, ingratitude spread right away. Dan shivered and shook till his bones rattled, but many of the city employees only laughed at him. One day, I remember, he tackled a clerk in the Public Works Department, who used to give up pretty regular, and, after the usual question, began to shiver. The clerk smiled. Dan shook till his hat fell off. The clerk took ten cents out of his pocket, handed it to Dan and said: "Poor man! Go and get a drink to warm yourself up." Wasn't that shameful? And yet, if it hadn't been for the civil service law, that clerk would be contributin' right along to this day.

The civil service law don't cover everything, however. There's lots of good jobs outside its clutch, and the men that get them are grateful every time. I'm not speakin' of Tammany Hall alone, remember! It's the same with the Republican Federal and State office-holders, and every organization that has or has had jobs to give out—except, of course, the Citizens' Union. The Cits held office only a couple of years and, knowin' that they would never be in again, each Cit officeholder held on for dear life to every dollar that came his way.

Some people say they can't understand what becomes of all the money that's collected for campaigns. They would understand fast enough if they were district leaders. There's never been half enough money to go around. Besides the expenses for meetin's, bands and all that, there's the bigger bill for the district workers who get men to the polls. These workers are mostly men who want to serve their country but can't get jobs in the city departments on account of the civil service law. They do the next best thing by keepin' track of the voters and seein' that they come to the polls and vote the right way. Some of these deservin' citizens have to make enough on registration and election days to keep them the rest of the year. Isn't it right that they should get a share of the campaign money?

Just remember that there's thirty-five Assembly districts in New York County, and thirty-six district leaders reachin' out for the Tammany dough-bag for somethin' to keep up the patriotism of ten thousand workers, and you wouldn't wonder that the cry for more, more, is goin' up from every district organization now and forevermore. Amen.

The Successful Politician
Does Not Drink

I HAVE explained how to succeed in politics. I want to
add that no matter how well you learn to play the political game, you won't make a lastin' success of it if
you're a drinkin' man. I never take a drop of any kind
of intoxicatin' liquor. I ain't no fanatic. Some of the
saloonkeepers are my best friends, and I don't mind
goin' into a saloon any day with my friends. But as a
matter of business I leave whisky and beer and the
rest of that stuff alone. As a matter of business, too, I
take for my lieutenants in my district men who don't
drink. I tried the other kind for several years, but it
didn't pay. They cost too much. For instance, I had
a young man who was one of the best hustlers in
town. He knew every man in the district, was popular everywhere and could induce a half-dead man to
come to the polls on election day. But, regularly, two
weeks before election, he started on a drunk, and I
had to hire two men to guard him day and night and

keep him sober enough to do his work. That cost a lot of money, and I dropped the young man after a while.

Maybe you think I'm unpopular with the saloon-keepers because I don't drink. You're wrong. The most successful saloonkeepers don't drink themselves and they understand that my temperance is a business proposition, just like their own. I have a saloon under my headquarters. If a saloonkeeper gets into trouble, he always knows that Senator Plunkitt is the man to help him out. If there is a bill in the Legislature makin' it easier for the liquor dealers, I am for it every time. I'm one of the best friends the saloon men have—but I don't drink their whisky. I won't go through the temperance lecture dodge and tell you how many bright young men I've seen fall victims to intemperance, but I'll tell you that I could name dozens—young men who had started on the road to statesmanship, who could carry their districts every time, and who could turn out any vote you wanted at the primaries. I honestly believe that drink is the greatest curse of the day, except, of course, civil service, and that it has driven more young men to ruin than anything except civil service examinations.

Look at the great leaders of Tammany Hall! No regular drinkers among them. Richard Croker's strongest drink was vichy. Charlie Murphy takes a glass of wine at dinner sometimes, but he don't go beyond that. A drinkin' man wouldn't last two weeks as leader of Tammany Hall. Nor can a man manage an assembly district long if he drinks. He's got to have a clear head all the time. I could name ten men who, in the last few years, lost their grip in their districts because they began drinkin'. There's now thirty-six district leaders in Tammany Hall, and I don't believe a half-dozen of them ever drink anything except at meals. People have got an idea that because the liquor men are with us in campaigns, our district leaders spend most of their time leanin' against bars. There couldn't be a wronger idea. The district leader makes a business of politics, gets his livin' out of it, and, in order to succeed, he's got to keep sober just like in any other business.

Just take as examples "Big Tim" and "Little Tim" Sullivan. They're known all over the country as the Bowery leaders and, as there's nothin' but saloons on the Bowery, people might think that they are hard drinkers. The fact is that neither of them has ever touched a drop of liquor in his life or even smoked a cigar. Still they don't make no pretenses of being better than anybody else, and don't go around deliverin' temperance lectures. Big Tim made money out of liquor—sellin' it to other people. That's the only way to get good out of liquor.

Look at all the Tammany heads of city departments! There's not a real drinkin' man in the lot. Oh, yes, there are some prominent men in the organization who drink sometimes, but they are not the men who have power. They're ornaments, fancy speakers and all that, who make a fine show behind the footlights, but ain't in it when it comes to directin' the city government and the Tammany organization. The men who sit in the executive committee room at Tammany Hall and direct things are men who celebrate on apollinaris or vichy. Let me tell you what I saw on election night in 1897, when the Tammany ticket swept the city: Up to 10 P.M. Croker, John F. Carroll, Tim Sullivan, Charlie Murphy, and myself sat in the committee room receivin' returns. When nearly all the city was heard from and we saw that Van Wyck was elected by a big majority, I invited the crowd to go across the street for a little celebration. A lot of small politicians followed us, expectin' to see magnums of champagne opened. The waiters in the restaurant expected it, too, and you never saw a more disgusted lot of waiters when they got our orders. Here's the orders: Croker, vichy and bicarbonate of soda; Carroll, seltzer lemonade; Sullivan, apollinaris; Murphy, vichy; Plunkitt, ditto. Before midnight we were all in bed, and next mornin' we were up bright and early attendin' to business, while other men were nursin' swelled heads. Is there anything the matter with temperance as a pure business proposition?

Bosses Preserve
the Nation

WHEN I retired from the Senate, I thought I would take a good, long rest, such a rest as a man needs who has held office for about forty years, and has held four different offices in one year and drawn salaries from three of them at the same time. Drawin' so many salaries is rather fatiguin', you know, and, as I said, I started out for a rest; but when I seen how things were goin' in New York State, and how a great big black shadow hung over us, I said to myself: "No rest for you, George. Your work ain't done. Your country still needs you and you mustn't lay down yet."

What was the great big black shadow? It was the primary election law, amended so as to knock out what are called the party bosses by lettin' in everybody at the primaries and givin' control over them to state officials. Oh, yes, that is a good way to do up the so-called bosses, but have you ever thought what would become of the country if the bosses were put out of business, and their places were taken by a lot of cart-tail orators and college graduates? It would mean chaos. It would be just like takin' a lot of dry-goods clerks and settin' them to run express trains on the New York Central Railroad. It makes my heart bleed to think of it. Ignorant people are always talkin' against party bosses, but just wait till the bosses are gone! Then, and not until then, will they get the right sort of epitaphs, as Patrick Henry or Robert Emmet said.

Look at the bosses of Tammany Hall in the last twenty years. What magnificent men! To them New York City owes pretty much all it is today. John Kelly, Richard Croker, and Charles F. Murphy— what names in American history compares with them, except Washington and Lincoln? They built up the grand Tammany organization, and the organization built up New York. Suppose the city had to depend for the last twenty years on irresponsible concerns like the Citizens' Union, where would it be now? You can make a pretty good guess if you recall the Strong and Low administrations when there was no boss, and the heads of departments were at odds all the time with each other, and the Mayor was at odds with the lot of them. They spent so much time in arguin' and makin' grandstand play, that the interests of the city were forgotten. Another administration of that kind would put New York back a quarter of a century.

Then see how beautiful a Tammany city government runs, with a so-called boss directin' the whole shootin' match! The machinery moves so noiseless that you wouldn't think there was any. If there's any differences of opinion, the Tammany leader settles them quietly, and his orders go every time. How nice it is for the people to feel that they can get up in the mornin' without bein' afraid of seein' in the papers that the Commissioner of Water Supply has sandbagged the Dock Commissioner, and that the Mayor and heads of the departments have been taken to the police court as witnesses! That's no joke. I remember that, under Strong, some commissioners came very near sandbaggin' one another.

Of course, the newspapers like the reform administration. Why? Because these administrations, with their daily rows, furnish as racy news as prizefights or divorce cases. Tammany don't care to get in the papers. It goes right along attendin' to business quietly and only wants to be let alone. That's one reason why the papers are against us.

Some papers complain that the bosses get rich while devotin' their lives to the interests of the city. What of it? If opportunities for turnin' an honest dollar comes their way, why shouldn't they take advantage of them, just as I have done? As I said, in another talk, there is honest graft and dishonest graft. The bosses go in for the former. There is so much of it in this big town that they would be fools to go in for dishonest graft.

Now, the primary election law threatens to do away with the boss and make the city government a menagerie. That's why I can't take the rest I counted on. I'm goin' to propose a bill for the next session of the legislature repealin' this dangerous law, and leavin' the primaries entirely to the organizations

themselves, as they used to be. Then will return the
good old times, when our district leaders could have
nice comfortable primary elections at some place selected by themselves and let in only men that they
approved of as good Democrats. Who is a better
judge of the Democracy of a man who offers his vote
than the leader of the district? Who is better equipped
to keep out undesirable voters?

The men who put through the primary law are the
same crowd that stand for the civil service blight and
they have the same objects in view—the destruction
of governments by party, the downfall of the constitution and hell generally.

Concerning Excise

ALTHOUGH I'm not a drinkin' man myself, I mourn with the poor liquor dealers of New York City, who are taxed and oppressed for the benefit of the farmers up the state. The Raines liquor law is infamous. It takes away nearly all the profits of the saloonkeepers, and then turns in a large part of the money to the State treasury to relieve the hayseeds from taxes. Ah, who knows how many honest, hard-workin' saloonkeepers have been driven to untimely graves by this law! I know personally of a half-dozen who committed suicide because they couldn't pay the enormous license fee, and I have heard of many others. Every time there is an increase of the fee, there is an increase in the suicide record of the city. Now, some of these Republican hayseeds are talkin' about makin' the liquor tax $1500, or even $2000 a year. That would mean the suicide of half of the liquor dealers in the city.

Just see how these poor fellows are oppressed all around! First, liquor is taxed in the hands of the manufacturer by the United States Government; second, the wholesale dealer pays a special tax to the government; third, the retail dealer is specially taxed by the United States Government; fourth, the retail dealer has to pay a big tax to the State government.

Now, liquor dealing is criminal or it ain't. If it's criminal, the men engaged in it ought to be sent to prison. If it ain't criminal, they ought to be protected and encouraged to make all the profit they honestly can. If it's right to tax a saloonkeeper $1000, it's right to put a heavy tax on dealers in other beverages—in milk, for instance—and make the dairymen pay up. But what a howl would be raised if a bill was introduced in Albany to compel the farmers to help support the State government! What would be said of a law that put a tax of, say $60 on a grocer, $150 on a dry-goods man, and $500 more if he includes the other goods that are kept in a country store?

If the Raines law gave the money extorted from the saloonkeepers to the city, there might be some excuse for the tax. We would get some benefit from it, but it gives a big part of the tax to local option localities where the people are always shoutin' that liquor dealin' is immoral. Ought these good people be subjected to the immoral influence of money taken from the saloons—tainted money? Out of respect for the tender consciences of these pious people, the Raines law ought to exempt them from all contamination from the plunder that comes from the saloon traffic. Say, mark that sarcastic. Some people who ain't used to fine sarcasm might think I meant it.

The Raines people make a pretense that the high license fee promotes temperance. It's just the other way around. It makes more intemperance and, what is as bad, it makes a monopoly in dram-shops. Soon the saloons will be in the hands of a vast trust, and any stuff can be sold for whisky or beer. It's gettin' that way already. Some of the poor liquor dealers in my district have been forced to sell wood alcohol for whisky, and many deaths have followed. A half-dozen men died in a couple of days from this kind of whisky which was forced down their throats by the high liquor tax. If they raise the tax higher, wood alcohol will be too costly, and I guess some dealers will have to get down to kerosene oil and add to the Rockefeller millions.

The way the Raines law divides the different classes of licenses is also an outrage. The sumptuous hotel saloons, with $10,000 paintin's and bricky-brac and Oriental splendors gets off easier than a shanty on the rocks, by the water's edge in my district where boatmen drink their grog, and the only ornaments is a three-cornered mirror nailed to the wall, and a chromo of the fight between Tom Hyer and Yankee Sullivan. Besides, a premium is put on places that sell liquor not to be drunk on the premises, but to be taken home. Now, I want to declare that from my experience in New York City, I would rather see rum sold in the dram-shops unlicensed, provided the rum is swallowed on the spot, than to encourage, by a low tax, "bucket-shops" from which the stuff is carried into the tenements at all hours of the day and night and make drunkenness and debauchery among the women and children. A "bucket-shop" in the tenement district means a cheap, so-called distillery, where raw spirits, poisonous colorin' matter and water are sold for brandy and whisky at ten cents a quart, and carried away in buckets and pitchers; I have always noticed that there are many undertakers wherever the "bucket-shop" flourishes, and they have no dull seasons.

I want it understood that I'm not an advocate of the liquor dealers or of drinkin'. I think every man would be better off if he didn't take any intoxicatin' drink at all, but as men will drink, they ought to have good stuff without impoverishin' themselves by goin' to fancy places and without riskin' death by goin' to poor places. The State should look after their interests as well as the interests of those who drink nothin' stronger than milk.

Now, as to the liquor dealers themselves. They ain't the criminals that cantin' hypocrites say they are. I know lots of them and I know that, as a rule, they're good honest citizens who conduct their business in a straight, honorable way. At a convention of the liquor dealers a few years ago, a big city official welcomed them on behalf of the city and said: "Go on elevatin' your standard higher and higher. Go on with your good work. Heaven will bless you!" That was puttin' it just a little strong, but the sentiment was all right and I guess the speaker went a bit further than he intended in his enthusiasm over meetin' such a fine set of men and, perhaps, dinin' with them.

A Parting Word on the Future of the Democratic Party in America

THE Democratic party of the nation ain't dead, though it's been givin' a lifelike imitation of a corpse for several years. It can't die while it's got Tammany for its backbone. The trouble is that the party's been chasin' after theories and stayin' up nights readin' books instead of studyin' human nature and actin' accordin', as I've advised in tellin' how to hold your district. In two Presidential campaigns, the leaders talked themselves red in the face about silver bein' the best money and gold bein' no good, and they tried to prove it out of books. Do you think the people cared for all that guff? No. They heartily indorsed what Richard Croker said at the Hoffman House one day in 1900. "What's the use of discussin' what's the best kind of money?" said Croker. "I'm in favor of all kinds of money—the more the better." See how a real Tammany statesman can settle in twenty-five words a problem that monopolized two campaigns!

Then imperialism. The Democratic party spent all its breath on that in the last national campaign. Its position was all right, sure, but you can't get people excited about the Philippines. They've got too much at home to interest them; they're too busy makin' a livin' to bother about the niggers in the Pacific. The party's got to drop all them put-you-to-sleep issues and come out in 1908 for somethin' that will wake the people up; somethin' that will make it worth while to work for the party.

There's just one issue that would set this country on fire. The Democratic party should say in the first plank of its platform: "We hereby declare, in national convention assembled, that the paramount issue now, always and forever, is the abolition of the iniquitous and villainous civil service laws which are destroyin' all patriotism, ruinin' the country and takin' away good jobs from them that earn them. We pledge ourselves, if our ticket is elected, to repeal those laws at once and put every civil service reformer in jail."

Just imagine the wild enthusiasm of the party, if that plank was adopted, and the rush of Republicans to join us in restorin' our country to what it was before this college professor's nightmare, called civil service reform, got hold of it! Of course, it would be all right to work in the platform some stuff about the tariff and sound money and the Philippines, as no platform seems to be complete without them, but they wouldn't count. The people would read only the first plank and then hanker for election day to come to put the Democratic party in office.

I see a vision. I see the civil service monster lyin'

flat on the ground. I see the Democratic party standin' over it with foot on its neck and wearin' the crown of victory. I see Thomas Jefferson lookin' out from a cloud and sayin': "Give him another sockdologer; finish him." And I see millions of men wavin' their hats and singin' "Glory Hallelujah!"

Strenuous Life of the Tammany District Leader

NOTE: *This chapter is based on extracts from Plunkitt's Diary and on my daily observation of the work of the district leader.* —W.L.R.

THE life of the Tammany district leader is strenuous. To his work is due the wonderful recuperative power of the organization.

One year it goes down in defeat and the prediction is made that it will never again raise its head. The district leader, undaunted by defeat, collects his scattered forces, organizes them as only Tammany knows how to organize, and in a little while the organization is as strong as ever.

No other politician in New York or elsewhere is exactly like the Tammany district leader or works as he does. As a rule, he has no business or occupation other than politics. He plays politics every day and night in the year, and his headquarters bears the inscription, "Never closed."

Everybody in the district knows him. Everybody knows where to find him, and nearly everybody goes to him for assistance of one sort or another, especially the poor of the tenements.

He is always obliging. He will go to the police courts to put in a good word for the "drunks and disorderlies" or pay their fines, if a good word is not effective. He will attend christenings, weddings, and funerals. He will feed the hungry and help bury the dead.

A philanthropist? Not at all. He is playing politics all the time.

Brought up in Tammany Hall, he has learned how to reach the hearts of the great mass of voters. He does not bother about reaching their heads. It is his belief that arguments and campaign literature have never gained votes.

He seeks direct contact with the people, does them good turns when he can, and relies on their not forgetting him on election day. His heart is always in his work, too, for his subsistence depends on its results.

If he holds his district and Tammany is in power, he is amply rewarded by a good office and the opportunities that go with it. What these opportunities are has been shown by the quick rise to wealth of so many Tammany district leaders. With the examples before him of Richard Croker, once leader of the Twentieth District; John F. Carroll, formerly leader of the Twenty-ninth; Timothy ("Dry Dollar") Sullivan, late leader of the Sixth, and many others, he can al-

ways look forward to riches and ease while he is going through the drudgery of his daily routine.

This is a record of a day's work by Plunkitt:

2 A.M.: Aroused from sleep by the ringing of his
doorbell; went to the door and found a bartender,
who asked him to go to the police station and bail out
a saloonkeeper who had been arrested for violating
the excise law. Furnished bail and returned to bed at
three o'clock.

6 A.M.: Awakened by fire engines passing his
house. Hastened to the scene of the fire, according to
the custom of the Tammany district leaders, to give
assistance to the fire sufferers, if needed. Met several
of his election district captains who are always under
orders to look out for fires, which are considered
great vote-getters. Found several tenants who had
been burned out, took them to a hotel, supplied them
with clothes, fed them, and arranged temporary
quarters for them until they could rent and furnish
new apartments.

8:30 A.M.: Went to the police court to look after his
constituents. Found six "drunks." Secured the dis-
charge of four by a timely word with the judge, and
paid the fines of two.

9 A.M.: Appeared in the Municipal District Court.
Directed one of his district captains to act as counsel
for a widow against whom dispossess proceedings
had been instituted and obtained an extension of
time. Paid the rent of a poor family about to be dis-
possessed and gave them a dollar for food.

11 A.M.: At home again. Found four men wait-
ing for him. One had been discharged by the Metro-

politan Railway Company for neglect of duty, and wanted the district leader to fix things. Another wanted a job on the road. The third sought a place on the Subway and the fourth, a plumber, was looking for work with the Consolidated Gas Company. The district leader spent nearly three hours fixing things for the four men, and succeeded in each case.

3 P.M.: Attended the funeral of an Italian as far as the ferry. Hurried back to make his appearance at the funeral of a Hebrew constituent. Went conspicuously to the front both in the Catholic church and the synagogue, and later attended the Hebrew confirmation ceremonies in the synagogue.

7 P.M.: Went to district headquarters and presided over a meeting of election district captains. Each captain submitted a list of all the voters in his district, reported on their attitude toward Tammany, suggested who might be won over and how they could be won, told who were in need, and who were in trouble of any kind and the best way to reach them. District leader took notes and gave orders.

8 P.M.: Went to a church fair. Took chances on everything, bought ice cream for the young girls and the children. Kissed the little ones, flattered their mothers and took their fathers out for something down at the corner.

9 P.M.: At the clubhouse again. Spent $10 on tickets for a church excursion and promised a subscription for a new church bell. Bought tickets for a baseball game to be played by two nines from his district. Listened to the complaints of a dozen pushcart peddlers who said they were persecuted by the police and as-

sured them he would go to Police Headquarters in the morning and see about it.

10:30 P.M.: Attended a Hebrew wedding reception and dance. Had previously sent a handsome wedding present to the bride.

12 P.M.: In bed.

That is the actual record of one day in the life of Plunkitt. He does some of the same things every day, but his life is not so monotonous as to be wearisome.

Sometimes the work of a district leader is exciting, especially if he happens to have a rival who intends to make a contest for the leadership at the primaries. In that case, he is even more alert, tries to reach the fires before his rival, sends out runners to look for "drunks and disorderlies" at the police stations, and keeps a very close watch on the obituary columns of the newspapers.

A few years ago there was a bitter contest for the Tammany leadership of the Ninth District between John C. Sheehan and Frank J. Goodwin. Both had had long experience in Tammany politics and both understood every move of the game.

Every morning their agents went to their respective headquarters before seven o'clock and read through the death notices in all the morning papers. If they found that anybody in the district had died, they rushed to the homes of their principals with the information and then there was a race to the house of the deceased to offer condolences, and, if the family were poor, something more substantial.

On the day of the funeral there was another contest. Each faction tried to surpass the other in the number and appearance of the carriages it sent to the funeral, and more than once they almost came to blows at the church or in the cemetery.

On one occasion the Goodwinites played a trick on their adversaries which has since been imitated in other districts. A well-known liquor dealer who had a considerable following died, and both Sheehan and Goodwin were eager to become his political heir by making a big showing at the funeral.

Goodwin managed to catch the enemy napping. He went to all the livery stables in the district, hired all the carriages for the day, and gave orders to two hundred of his men to be on hand as mourners.

Sheehan had never had any trouble about getting all the carriages that he wanted, so he let the matter go until the night before the funeral. Then he found that he could not hire a carriage in the district.

He called his district committee together in a hurry and explained the situation to them. He could get all the vehicles he needed in the adjoining district, he said, but if he did that, Goodwin would rouse the voters of the Ninth by declaring that he (Sheehan) had patronized foreign industries.

Finally, it was decided that there was nothing to do but to go over to Sixth Avenue and Broadway for carriages. Sheehan made a fine turnout at the funeral, but the deceased was hardly in his grave before Goodwin raised the cry of "Protection to home industries," and denounced his rival for patronizing livery-stable keepers outside of his district. The cry had its effect in the primary campaign. At all events, Goodwin was elected leader.

A recent contest for the leadership of the Second

District illustrated further the strenuous work of the Tammany district leaders. The contestants were Patrick Divver, who had managed the district for years, and Thomas F. Foley.

Both were particularly anxious to secure the large Italian vote. They not only attended all the Italian christenings and funerals, but also kept a close lookout for the marriages in order to be on hand with wedding presents.

At first, each had his own reporter in the Italian quarter to keep track of the marriages. Later, Foley conceived a better plan. He hired a man to stay all day at the City Hall marriage bureau, where most Italian couples go through the civil ceremony, and telephone to him at his saloon when anything was doing at the bureau.

Foley had a number of presents ready for use and, whenever he received a telephone message from his man, he hastened to the City Hall with a ring or a watch or a piece of silver and handed it to the bride with his congratulations. As a consequence, when Divver got the news and went to the home of the couple with his present, he always found that Foley had been ahead of him. Toward the end of the campaign, Divver also stationed a man at the marriage bureau and then there were daily foot races and fights between the two heelers.

Sometimes the rivals came into conflict at the deathbed. One night a poor Italian peddler died in Roosevelt Street. The news reached Divver and Foley about the same time, and as they knew the family of the man was destitute, each went to an undertaker and brought him to the Roosevelt Street tenement.

The rivals and the undertakers met at the house and an altercation ensued. After much discussion the Divver undertaker was selected. Foley had more carriages at the funeral, however, and he further impressed the Italian voters by paying the widow's rent for a month, and sending her half a ton of coal and a barrel of flour.

The rivals were put on their mettle toward the end of the campaign by the wedding of a daughter of one of the original Cohens of the Baxter Street region. The Hebrew vote in the district is nearly as large as the Italian vote, and Divver and Foley set out to capture the Cohens and their friends.

They stayed up nights thinking what they would give the bride. Neither knew how much the other was prepared to spend on a wedding present, or what form it would take; so spies were employed by both sides to keep watch on the jewelry stores, and the jewelers of the district were bribed by each side to impart the desired information.

At last Foley heard that Divver had purchased a set of silver knives, forks and spoons. He at once bought a duplicate set and added a silver tea service. When the presents were displayed at the home of the bride, Divver was not in a pleasant mood and he charged his jeweler with treachery. It may be added that Foley won at the primaries.

One of the fixed duties of a Tammany district leader is to give two outings every summer, one for the men of his district and the other for the women and children, and a beefsteak dinner and a ball every winter. The scene of the outings is, usually, one of the groves along the Sound.

The ambition of the district leader on these occasions is to demonstrate that his men have broken all records in the matter of eating and drinking. He gives out the exact number of pounds of beef, poultry, butter, etc., that they have consumed and professes to know how many potatoes and ears of corn have been served.

According to his figures, the average eating record of each man at the outing is about ten pounds of beef, two or three chickens, a pound of butter, a half peck of potatoes, and two dozen ears of corn. The drinking records, as given out, are still more phenomenal. For some reason, not yet explained, the district leader thinks that his popularity will be greatly increased if he can show that his followers can eat and drink more than the followers of any other district leader.

The same idea governs the beefsteak dinners in the winter. It matters not what sort of steak is served or how it is cooked; the district leader considers only the question of quantity, and when he excels all others in this particular, he feels, somehow, that he is a bigger man and deserves more patronage than his associates in the Tammany Executive Committee.

As to the balls, they are the events of the winter in the extreme East Side and West Side society. Mamie and Maggie and Jennie prepare for them months in advance, and their young men save up for the occasion just as they save for the summer trips to Coney Island.

The district leader is in his glory at the opening of the ball. He leads the cotillion with the prettiest woman present—his wife, if he has one, permitting—and spends almost the whole night shaking

hands with his constituents. The ball costs him a pretty penny, but he has found that the investment pays.

By these means the Tammany district leader reaches out into the homes of his district, keeps watch not only on the men, but also on the women and children; knows their needs, their likes and dislikes, their troubles and their hopes, and places himself in a position to use his knowledge for the benefit of his organization and himself. Is it any wonder that scandals do not permanently disable Tammany and that it speedily recovers from what seems to be crushing defeat?